RETHINKING MARRIAGE

RETHINKING MARRIAGE
Public and Private Perspectives

edited by
Christopher Clulow

Foreword by
Jack Dominian

London
KARNAC BOOKS

First published in 1993 by
H. Karnac (Books) Ltd.
58 Gloucester Road
London SW7 4QY

British Library Cataloguing in Publication Data.

Rethinking Marriage: Public and Private
Perspectives. — (Tavistock Institute of
Marital Studies Series)
I. Clulow, Christopher F. II. Series
306.81
ISBN 1-85575-046-5

Printed in Great Britain by BPCC Wheatons Ltd, Exeter

CONTENTS

BIOGRAPHICAL NOTES

EILEEN BERTIN began her training as a counsellor in 1981 with the National Marriage Guidance Council (as Relate was then known). She completed her training in 1984 and has continued as a practitioner with Relate ever since. She further trained as an Education Worker and worked with groups of young people and those preparing for marriage. She has been a trainer for the National Health Service, offering counselling skills to medical professionals, and a tutor for Adult Education in counselling, and she has trained professionals from other disciplines. She is currently a trainer and supervisor for Relate and lives in Bushey with her husband and two daughters.

PAUL BROWN is a chartered clinical and occupational psychologist. After graduating from the University of Durham in 1961 he qualified at the Institute of Psychiatry, University of London, and then spent thirteen years in the National Health Service specializing in the treatment of behavioural difficulties and sexual problems. During this time he held an Honorary Lectureship at the University of Birmingham, was an external examiner at the Tavistock Clinic, and was Honorary Secretary of the Clinical Division of the British Psychological Society.

Dr Brown now maintains an international private practice based in London. Clinically he specializes in marital and sexual difficulties; organizationally he is especially interested in the selection and development of senior individuals in commercial organizations and is Senior European Psychologist for KRW International, based in the United States. He holds an Honorary Lectureship at Goldsmith's College, University of London, and he has published *Treat Yourself to Sex*—a best-seller—and *Managing Meetings*.

CHRISTOPHER CLULOW is the Director of the Tavistock Institute of Marital Studies where he works as a marital therapist, teacher, and researcher. He also chairs the Commission on Marriage and Interpersonal Relations of the International Union of Family Organisations. He has published extensively on marriage and family issues, including, together with Janet Mattinson, a Penguin paperback for the general reader, *Marriage Inside Out*. His particular working interests have been the transition to parenthood and the management of divorce. After graduating in Economics at the University of Exeter, he completed post-graduate social work training and joined the Probation Service for five years. He has worked for the Tavistock Institute of Marital Studies since 1974, and he is a member of the recently formed Society of Psychoanalytical Marital Psychotherapists.

WARREN COLMAN is a senior marital psychotherapist at the Tavistock Institute of Marital Studies, an associate professional member of the Society of Analytical Psychology, and a member of the recently formed Society of Psychoanalytical Marital Psychotherapists. He graduated in English and Sociology at Keele University in 1973 and worked in the voluntary social work field before qualifying as a social worker and as a Diploma member of the Institute of Psychotherapy and Counselling (Westminster Pastoral Foundation). He also worked in a social services department before joining the Tavistock Institute of Marital Studies in 1982. He has published a number of papers on individual and marital psychotherapy, and a book, *On Call: The Work of a Telephone Helpline for Child Abusers.* He now co-ordinates the Institute's Diploma in Marital Psychotherapy training and a training programme for family counsellors in Sweden. He is in private practice as a psychotherapist and Jungian analyst in London and St Albans.

PENNY MANSFIELD is the Deputy Director of One Plus One, Marriage and Partnership Research, at the Central Middlesex Hospital. She has previously undertaken research at University. A research sociologist, she has written a number of articles and has contributed to books. She is co-author (with Jean Collard) of *The Beginning of the Rest of Your Life?*—the first book describing the marriages of a group of couples who have been followed in the early years of marriage. A sequel— *Person: Partner: Parent*—is being produced with colleagues Fiona McAllister and Jean Collard.

SUSIE ORBACH is a psychotherapist and writer. With Luise Eichenbaum she co-founded The Women's Therapy Centre in London in 1976 and The Women's Therapy Centre Institute in New York in 1981. She lectures extensively in Europe and North America, and she has a practice seeing individuals and couples and acting as consultant to organizations.

Her books include *Fat is a Feminist Issue, Fat is a Feminist Issue 2,* and *Hunger Strike: The Anorectic's Struggle as a Metaphor for Our Age.* With Luise Eichenbaum she has written *Understanding Women: A Feminist Psychoanalytic Account, What Do Women Want? Exploding the Myth of Dependency,* and *Bittersweet: Love, Competition and Envy in Women's Relationships.* She writes a monthly column for *Guardian Weekend* on emotional issues. She lives in London with her partner and their two children.

MICHAEL SADGROVE is Canon Residentiary, Precenter, and Vice Provost of Coventry Cathedral. A Londoner by birth, he read Mathematics, Philosophy, and Theology at Oxford University. After ordination, he taught Old Testament Studies at Salisbury and Wells Theological College, after which he became Vicar of Alnwick in Northumberland. He moved to his present post in 1987. He is married to a Relate counsellor and has four children.

MARTIN RICHARDS is Reader in Human Development at Cambridge University and Head of the Centre for Family Research (formerly Child Care and Development Group). He has researched extensively in the areas of parent–child relations and divorce and marriage. His books include *Sexual Arrangements: Marriage and Affairs* (with Janet Reibstein), *Divorce Matters* (with Jackie Burgoyne and Roger Ormrod), *Infancy: The World of the Newborn*, and *Children in Social Worlds* (edited with Paul Light).

FOREWORD

Jack Dominian

Marriage would have to be invented, if it did not already exist—writes Christopher Clulow at the end of this book, which concerns itself with the interaction between the inner and the outer worlds of current marriage.

Historically, the world of marriage has been subject to constant change. Today its inner reality is influenced by its longevity, the end of the absolute link between sexual intercourse and procreation, the emancipation of women, and a hundred years of psychological knowledge, which has opened adult intimacy to reflect the relationship between child and parent.

All these changes impinge on the inner world of marriage and stand against tradition, the law, morality, religion, and the expectations of previous generations. The interaction between the social and the psychological, the outer and the inner, is lived in every marriage, and the stresses and strains make the stuff of its contemporary life.

The results can be both exciting and challenging as well as confusing and damaging. On the one hand new heights of happiness are achieved by couples, and on the other there is widespread marital breakdown, with all the disillusion and suffering that it contains.

This book brings together a group of specialists who attempt to describe the process of interaction between the inner and personal and the outer and social. They illustrate what is happening to current marriage, particularly in its daily intimate experience. They do not attempt to offer expert solutions. They describe practice as they see it.

The book is a valuable study to help the clarification of the complex world of contemporary marriage, particularly as it stresses the dynamic aspects of the marital relationship which are the key to its present aspirations. It is a study that informs both the expert and the lay reader, helping to make sense of the necessary diverse realities that make up marriage today.

RETHINKING MARRIAGE

Looking for help

Eileen Bertin

Portrait of a problem

John and Mary were in their mid-thirties and had been married for four years when they came for help.[1] The presenting problem was their concern over the lack of sex in their relationship and their constant rows.

It had not always been like that. When they first married, their relationship had been idyllic. John thought he had found the perfect partner in Mary. They were both Irish, both brought up Catholic, and their assumption was that they would understand each other totally.

John was the middle one of three boys. His mother devoted her life to her family and her home. His father held a position in the Royal Ulster Constabulary, which meant that security was always an important issue: no one outside the family could be trusted. The net effect was to make the family tight, close, and very careful. When John was four years old, he was very ill and spent several months in hospital. He became "precious" and developed an especially close relationship with his mother. He recovered well from his illness, and, like his brothers, he was

1

very sporty. Keeping fit continued to be important to him. His family were active Catholics, and during his teenage years John wanted to become a priest. He was the golden boy in the family. He believed that, as a good Catholic son, he should enter the ranks of the professions and become a priest, a doctor, or a lawyer. In his late teens he was unable to reconcile his sexuality with his desire to become a priest, and so he became a lawyer.

Mary was the eldest of five girls. Her mother had always worked. Her father, too, was a hard-working, rather distant man, who was not at all affectionate to his daughters. Mary went to a convent school, where she did as well as she was expected to—by which she meant that girls in her family were not expected to have a career, but to become good wives and mothers. Hers was a loose-knit, extended family, but she grew up without much mixing with the rest of the community. Her mother wanted her to conform to her ideas of what a good girl should be, and many of her sayings and edicts lingered on: "least said, soonest mended"; "you'll be better before you wed"; "self-praise is no praise"; and so on. Mary was a plump child with a poor self-image. When she left school, she went abroad to stay with relatives. She came back to England to go to university, where she gained a degree as a mature student.

When John met Mary, he was impressed by her self-discipline in achieving higher education, and he admired her self-containment. Mary was attracted to John's strength, his warmth, and his ability to show affection.

After they married, Mary put on more weight, and John found her less attractive sexually—mostly because he felt this displayed a lack of the self-discipline he had so much admired. He encouraged her to lose weight, and to please him she did so very effectively. It was after a visit to the slimming clinic, when he was overwhelmed by her perfect body, that John made love to Mary and their child was conceived.

John had never wanted children, and he was horrified that Mary was pregnant. She, on the other hand, was delighted; she wanted children very much. Their differences at this time were exacerbated by their financial position, as John had just made a career change to start his own business, and he needed Mary's financial support. Mary was not well during the pregnancy. She had high blood pressure. She avoided doctors and

developed toxaemia. She "managed" by being fiercely independent and continuing to work until the last possible moment.
The birth of the baby went badly wrong. John was with her
during the delivery, and it was a very emotional experience for
them both. Mary almost died.

The experience changed Mary. She began to value herself
and her life in a different way. She lost the weight she had put
on during pregnancy. Although she continued to be unwell, she
managed the baby and the home; and she went back to work
within three months. This enabled John to concentrate on his
new business and on providing for his family. He was delighted
with the baby and was surprised at the depth and power of his
love for the child.

However, the marriage deteriorated as John increased his
demands that Mary be self-sufficient in their relationship. Sex
came to an end between them. They were considering separating when they approached Relate, a national counselling
agency particularly geared to helping couples, for help.

A counselling response

When I first met John and Mary, I was struck by their appearance. Mary was petite, slim, and very glamorous; John was
well-presented and articulate. He did most of the talking and
explained how embarrassed he felt at having to go to an agency
to sort out his personal problems. Mary was desperate for some
kind of resolution. She was not prepared to acquiesce to his
demands for her to be perfect any longer and was worried that
he was really asking her to be someone other than she was.

Expectations

The early sessions of counselling focused on John and Mary's
expectations of each other, the marriage, and their belief that
because they shared a culture they would understand each
other totally. As we explored their backgrounds, it gradually
became apparent to them what a fundamentally false assump-

tion this was. Differences in their learned patterns of relating became more obvious: he came from a tight-knit, enclosed family, where everything was discussed and debated; she came from a loose-knit, extended family, where nothing was discussed, but there was an edict for every situation. His learned pattern was to discuss everything at length; hers was to say little. In the counselling room I would often find myself in discussion with John while Mary took the role of observer. They talked to each other through me. I encouraged him to listen more to her needs and her to make her needs more explicit. The first real breakthrough in the counselling came when they began to understand and accept their differences in communication.

Control

Mary changed the rules in the relationship after the birth of their baby and no longer acquiesced to John's control. The more she resisted, the more controlling he became. He was almost obsessional in his need to have the house immaculately clean and tidy, and for Mary to be "perfect". The only control Mary felt she had was the power of veto: she could withhold acquiescence.

John's fear of being out of control can be understood as stemming from his early life, when the family's safety and survival depended on everything being under control because of his father's job. The message he received as a child was: "trust no one; check everything". He learned that to be out of control was to risk life. The lesson to "stay in control in order to survive" masked other feelings. As a young child, John's early needs for dependency had not been adequately met. What Malan (1979) would call John's "central and recurring pain" was exacerbated by his illness at the age of four. During counselling he got in touch with some anger towards his parents about the situation he had grown up in, and he gained insight into why he and his brothers had distanced themselves from their motherland, Ireland.

Why had Mary acquiesced for so long, and why had she been attracted to this controlling man? In her family she had always obeyed edicts. She felt she had never been treated as an individual and described how, when she was a teenager, her mother made her walk behind her when they went to Mass because she was plump. This was her mother's way of encouraging her to lose weight. Mary's "central and recurring pain" was her belief that love is conditional. When Mary was pregnant and vulnerable, she could not risk saying "I need", because she felt that John's love for her was conditional on her being self-sufficient, independent, and "perfect".

John's early life experience had led him to hold the unconscious belief that not to be in control was to put survival at stake. Consequently, he could neither depend on Mary for emotional and financial support as the business struggled, nor could he offer her the opportunity to depend on him while she was in the vulnerable state of pregnancy. The actual threat to life during birth reinforced the anxiety. Their unconscious fear of dependency provided a "fit" between their individual defensive systems.

The second breakthrough in counselling came with an understanding of their shared need to control and be controlled. John and Mary had repeatedly asked for a task to be set for them to complete between sessions. Having resisted on several occasions, I eventually capitulated, giving them a simple communication exercise to do. When they came to the next session, they had not done it. I was irritated and heard myself chastising them for demanding homework and then not doing it. I discovered I had been put in the position of controller. In the transference I had become the "controlling mother", and they had rebelled. They were much amused by this link and took its significance on board. They recognized, in their interaction, ways in which they responded to each other as if they were controlling parents. From this point on communication became easier and much more effective, and they ceased to talk through me.

Sexuality

The issue of control also affected their sexual relationship. Sex had been wonderful when they first met. Both had felt free to enjoy themselves. But after they were married and Mary became fatter, John became less interested in her. Mary would become very angry that things had to be perfect in order for John to be "turned on". Even affectionate cuddles between them became less frequent, so Mary was rarely "in the mood". There was also a real fear of another pregnancy and the pain and damage that might accompany it.

There were also fears surrounding sex itself. Mary had been brought up in an almost totally female environment: her four sisters, her mother, the nuns at school. The only men in her life were her father and the priest. She and her sisters were encouraged to hide their sexuality from their father, who gave little of the necessary approval for his daughters' development. She described how, when she left home for the first time to work abroad, her father had shaken hands with her. Her mother also appeared uncomfortable with sexuality and had a saying about menstruation that "women needed to bleed, or else they ended up in an asylum". Thus, Mary's sex education experience was very restricted; messages were implicit and surrounded by folklore.

John, reciprocally, was brought up in an almost totally male environment: his brothers, his father, an all-boys' school, and the priests. The only woman in his life was his mother, who gave John the impression that sex was a bad and dirty thing. It was the only subject not discussed in the family. During counselling he was sure his history had no bearing on the present. He believed he had freed himself from his repressive upbringing by giving up his Catholicism and being promiscuous, fully exploring his sexuality. Yet he married Mary.

Mary believed that John was very experienced when they met and that he could help her inexperience. Sexual difficulties were therefore a particular blow to each of them. As their counsellor, I asked how they were managing their sexual feelings, given that nothing was happening between them. At the time I had no idea of the impact of the question on John. During the following week he wrote a very long letter to Mary, with a copy to me, detailing the torment he had put himself through whilst he was growing up as he battled with his sexual urges and his Catholic belief. In the end sex had won, and he had tried to "desensitize" himself against guilt by promiscuity. In that last session I had given him permission to have sexual feelings. In that moment he realized that, until then, he had been continuing to react against his upbringing, and that he had viewed Mary as his disapproving mother. He located his own control and sexual guilt in her. Mary found all this a bit perplexing and became angry with him.

It was also becoming clear that sex was not experienced as interaction but as self-centred satisfaction. It was sex without intimacy, perhaps because loss of control and dependency are essential components of intimacy. If John were to allow Mary to express her sexual needs, and he were to attempt to meet them, he would be allowing her to become dependent on him. If Mary were to allow John to see her sexual needs, she would no longer be self-sufficient in his eyes, and she would risk his withdrawal from her.

Although nothing became magically better between them, there was a sense of a new beginning and hope. John began to reorientate himself in his relationships with women and with himself. Mary assumed more power in the marriage. They felt they had come a long way, and they decided to end counselling to see if they could live with what they had achieved. I offered further counselling at a later date if they chose, modelling that they could be both independent of and dependent on me in the future.

Learning interdependence

Significant processes in the counselling work were as follows:

- helping John and Mary to separate from each other emotionally as they worked through the realization that they had been re-enacting their pasts in the marriage; this involved recognizing the transferences operating between them and with me, and their fears of dependency;

- helping them to accept their differences and to give up the illusion of perfect understanding between them as the model of a good marriage;

- encouraging interdependence, easing the defence of self-sufficiency without inviting a dependency that negated either partner.

Where interdependence can be achieved, security and intimacy within relationships can provide the foundations for gratifying experience. If partners can, on the one hand, feel sufficiently supported in the task of home-making or providing for the family and, on the other, find sufficient satisfaction of mutual need and pleasure in the regressive play of lovemaking, dependence can be tolerated, and the relationship can develop creatively. However, where there is quite severe frustration or insecurity in childhood, a return to a loving relationship can re-awaken buried dependency needs, or the fear of them, in all their intensity. The very partner who at first seemed self-sufficient and undemanding may become the more demanding of the two in the process of struggling with an infantile desire to control the loved person absolutely and make him or her pro-vide what is needed. Interdependence can then be very difficult.

The struggle for interdependence involves rethinking mar-riage, but it is the hallmark of a successful relationship, recognized by poets and marital therapists alike. "Let there be spaces in your togetherness", breathes Kahlil Gibran in his poem about marriage (1926). And, more prosaically:

> The failure to achieve a minimum of emotional independ-ence is one of the main causes of marital breakdown. . . . Emotional dependence is often accompanied by a variable degree of anger and hostility. Independence, autonomy and self-control are the prized characteristics of emotional maturity. Their absence restricts, inhibits and places the sufferer in the hands of others for survival. [Dominian, 1968, p. 43]

Or again:

> The attainment of this adult interdependency requires a depth and intimacy of involvement from each partner which matches in intensity the exclusive, dependent rela-tions of childhood. [Pincus, 1960, p. 31]

NOTE

1. I am very grateful to John and Mary for willingly giving me permission to use this material, a decision they made in the hope that it would be helpful to others. Factual details have been altered to conceal their identity.

CHAPTER ONE

Rethinking marriage

Christopher Clulow

There are times in most marriages when a crisis, and sometimes an absence of crisis, forces the partners into a reappraisal of their relationship. Predictable passages—setting up home, starting a family, children leaving home, ailing parents—and unexpected events—a sudden illness, an affair, relocation at work, redundancy—can destabilize the balance of married life and demand changes. They interact with the long-standing psychological traits of individuals and their partnerships to bind some couples to-gether while blowing others apart. This interaction between external events and inner-world realities results in varied out-comes, confirming Anthony Powell's dictum that "it is not what happens to people that is significant, but what they think happens to them" (Powell, 1971). Couples may be so disturbed by their interpretation of events that one or both partners come to believe they have a marital problem for which they need help. Or, perhaps, the problem they have is, indeed, "marital", for it is presented in the context of the couple and not as a request for individual help, or help with a child, or assistance in managing other vicissitudes of life that can affect marriage.

The couple described in the Prologue understood their problem to lie in the marriage. A traumatic birth, coupled with financial anxieties occasioned by the new responsibilities of parenthood, acted as triggers that demanded long-standing patterns of relating to be rethought. The counselling response highlighted tensions associated with differences, expectations, sexuality, and controlling behaviour and defined the task for the partners as one of learning to become interdependent.

Within the microcosm of this particular marriage are contained themes that recur in the wider debate about the state of marriage, and that form the subject of this book—companionate values that encourage the search for a soul-mate in contemporary marriage, the disillusion that follows disappointed expectations, the impact of religious teaching on human sexuality, dynamics of dependency and control between men and women, the tension between individual and collective agendas, the quest for personal integrity and moral consensus, and so on.

Therapeutic responses to marital problems attend to the interaction between partners, examining the conscious and unconscious assumptions that govern their intercourse. The juxtaposition between past and present, between inner and outer realities, provides a focus for interpreting marital conflict. Enactments in the course of therapy, reports from the marital front, and recounted fragments of past life are the main objects of the therapist's attention. In this sense the therapist is primarily concerned with the personal worlds of couples and less interested in the social structures and cultures within which their lives are played out.

There are good reasons for this. The object of therapeutic endeavour is to empower people to take responsibility for their lives so they become the agents, not the subjects, of change. It is not part of the enterprise to define them as victims of the social system, although, to greater or lesser extents, environmental factors will have an impact on their lives. The relevant system for the marital therapist is the couple relationship, and enactments in other social contexts (primarily that of the therapist/couple relationship) will be linked with this central concern.

Of course, focusing on one area restricts the field of vision. This has been a source of criticism of couple therapy insofar as it blinds therapists to the part they play in constructing (as well as responding to) marital issues. For example, Morgan (1992) questions whether the work of marriage guidance is simply to respond to the needs of couples and suggests that the focus of the "clinical gaze" (a term he borrows from Foucault) is an active part of the process of defining what constitutes a marital problem. In other words, the relational values of counselling dictate as well as respond to notions of what constitutes a "good" marriage.

Certainly, explanations for marital problems will be sought by therapists in personal, not public, terms. This corresponds with the inclination of most partners seeking help, who will tend to blame either themselves or each other for the problems they have. The financial or "mother-in-law" complaints of yester-year have been succeeded by those to do with communication difficulties (sometimes over the same subjects) from today's couples. But there is still a sizeable group of "don't knows" who wonder how their marriages compare with those of others, and for whom the knowledge that they are not alone in their experience would come as a profound relief.

From my standpoint as a marital therapist, the interconnections between inner and outer realities are the stuff of marriage. In this context it is, for me, as absurd to consider psychological factors in isolation from social environment as it would be to regard social systems as being made up of roles rather than people. In the words of social scientist Peter Marris (1992), "the experience of attachment, which so profoundly influences the growth of personality, is itself both the product of a culture, and a determinant of how that culture will be reproduced in the next generation" (pp. 79–80). Although he was writing with reference to relationships between parents and children, his words can be applied with equal weight to relationships between partners in marriage.

It is therefore legitimate to address a therapist's questions not only to the predicament of particular couples, but also to the public face of marriage itself. This may help in rethinking the *institution* as well as the *relationship* of marriage. Why, for example, is it necessary to rethink marriage at all at this particular point in history? Is there a problem—and, if so, for whom? If there is a problem, what explanations are being proffered? And what remedies do these explanations imply?

Most of the contributions in this book accept that there is a problem and address themselves to the nature of the problem. This is not surprising, since, for many of the contributors, it is the problems in marriage that present themselves for their professional attention. Despite some accounts of successful couple relationships (see, for example, Housden & Goodchild, 1992), there has yet to be conducted in this country a systematic study of what makes marriages work. Nevertheless, an examination of the problems in marriage is illuminating because it suggests answers to a fundamental question—one that underlies every contribution to this book: what is marriage for?

What is marriage for?

It is common knowledge that the institution of marriage—the legally sanctioned union of one man with one woman, voluntarily entered into, to the exclusion of all others—has been weakened in the past two decades by high divorce rates, falling marriage rates, and a growing tendency for couples to eschew marriage in favour of living together and, for an increasing number of parents, to raise children out of wedlock. These changing patterns of family life have provided the impetus for the current debate about marriage. But why should such trends be regarded as problematic? If the current emphasis is on marriage as relationship rather than marriage as institution, should not the organization of family relationships be a private matter? And if these arrangements are to be regarded as matters of public concern, how can we be sure that they are problems in themselves and not symptomatic of other, more deep-seated, social ills?

Historians (see, for example, Stone, 1992) point out that the dilemmas we face are nothing new. Just as the nature of marriage changes over time for individuals, so it does for societies. In the twelfth and thirteenth centuries, the essence of marriage was held, by no less an authority than the Pope, to be simply the verbal exchange of vows by consenting adults in the presence of two witnesses. In England and Wales, folk ritual competed with formal procedures even after the Hardwicke Marriage Act gave the Established Church a monopoly over weddings in 1753. To put our present law into historical perspective, the civil registration of marriages dates back only to 1836. The formal institution of marriage can therefore be seen as the product of a relatively recent historical cycle.

Historians are not the only ones to dampen assertions that the present predicament of marriage is unique. Demographers observe that there are remarkable similarities in family trends between different western countries (see, for example, Dumon, 1991), inviting speculation that there might be some kind of "continental drift" in the western world towards legally recognized private contracts between couples, and that this could represent evolutionary development rather than a degenerative cycle. If that uni-directional flow argument is accepted (and it is not one advanced by Dumon or his colleagues in the European Observatory on National Family Policies), concern about changes in marriage can be regarded as no more than the protests of those who wish to preserve old skins to contain the new wine of couple relationships. This perspective is prominent amongst the literally minded, who will point out that the sole reason for divorce is marriage. By doing so, they raise a serious question about whether the problem is not so much with *divorce* as with *marriage*.

Divorce at the scale we have today is, however, a new phenomenon for the United Kingdom. While remarriage has always been common, the difference today is that it is most likely to be preceded by marriage breakdown than by the death of a spouse. The rate of change in this respect has been particularly rapid in the last fifty years, but the public response to it has been remarkably constant. A *Royal Commission on Marriage and Divorce* published in 1955 expressed concern about the rate of marriage breakdown in terms very similar to those expressed in the divorce debate today. Perhaps the one difference to emerge is that while the Commission accepted the desirability of equality between men and women in marriage, and recognized the practical pressures of "housing shortages" and "the complexities of modern life", the suspicion of blame was laid at the feet of couples who might be taking the "duties

and responsibilities of marriage less seriously than formerly".
While that view is still voiced today, the lack of social stigma
attached to divorce suggests a different mood.

So what is marriage for as we approach the millennium?
Michael Sadgrove draws attention later in this book to the re-
ordering of the reasons for which marriage exists as listed in
the 1980 *Alternative Service Book of the Church of England.*
The procreation of children, which appeared as the primary
reason in the 1662 *Book of Common Prayer*, has been relegated
to third place. The "remedy against sin"—in other words, the
regulation of sexual behaviour—stays in second place, but is
expressed in very different language, which embraces, rather
than wards off, human sexuality. In first place comes mutual
comfort, help, and fidelity. In social science terms, this primary
purpose is equated with *companionate values* in contemporary
marriage.

How well do these purposes stand up today?

Companionship

In chapter two, Martin Richards traces the development of
companionate marriage over recent history and highlights
some of the contradictions inherent in it. From historical
sources relating to middle-class marriages in Britain, he
illustrates how key issues in the debate about marriage are
not new but show continuity over time. He argues that it is less
the vows people make than the assumptions they hold about
marriage that cause problems, and he concludes that companionate marriage contains the seeds of its own destruction.

Evidence of companionate values in marriage is not hard to
find. In professional circles, states of physiological arousal,
facial expressions, and degrees of emotional accessibility become the visible predictors of success or failure in marriage
(Gottman, 1991). The focus of attention is on the couple, or the
individuals who make up the couple, rather than on the environment in which they live out their lives together. Most
couples agree with this focus. When a marriage breaks down,
explanations will be sought in personal terms—infidelity, betrayal, isolation, violence, boredom, emptiness, loss of self. The

social, insofar as it features, extends only to the relationship between the partners and, perhaps, specific third parties within and outside the family circle.

The picture is confirmed in attitude surveys. A Gallup Poll conducted in England in 1990 asked respondents what qualities they thought most important in a marriage partner. In rank order they were as follows: being faithful, caring and loving, having a sense of humour, understanding and tolerance, unselfishness, being prepared to listen, kind, hard-working, home-loving, fun to talk to, sexually responsive, good-looking/physically attractive.

Two points of interest emerge from the list: (1) the emphasis placed on the quality of the relationship; (2) the high level of agreement between men and women about rank ordering (sex being the one variable that was more important for men than for women). Emotional support, companionship and conversation were of greater importance than shared social background or agreement on politics and religion. But women were three times as likely as men to say they received too little emotional support from their partners. And, in contrast to predictions being made just 25 years ago, women—not men—are today the more anxious of the sexes to leave their marriages. Here lies one explanation for the current instability of marriage: a burden of thwarted expectations, which has led "intolerable disappointment" to replace "irretrievable breakdown" as the ground for divorce—and especially for women.

Another explanation for the instability of marriage in present times, and one that appears to contradict the expectations argument, is that couples come under pressure in their relationships because there are so few social reference points against which to check out their personal experiences. The contradiction may be more apparent than real, for when traditional landmarks disappear, the search for something to replace them becomes intense. Thus, paradoxically, the more intensely private people become in their marriages, the less of a window they have into the domestic lives of others, the more than usually susceptible they will be to images presented to them of "normal" family life.

This thesis lies at the heart of Penny Mansfield's contribution in chapter three, and it is no accident that she selects the part played by sociologists and therapists in constructing marriage (at least in the eyes of their audiences) as being of particular interest. Each of these two professions creates powerful images of marriage that have direct effects on couples.

Ironically, those working primarily in the private domain have been as active as any in constructing images of marriage. My own stance as a marital psychotherapist contains a particular perspective on conflict in marriage, which I share with colleagues at the Tavistock Institute of Marital Studies. We tend to regard conflict as holding potential for personal growth and development, and the therapeutic enterprise as one of exploring and trying to make sense of tensions that are particular to different partnerships. Whether this attitude works to ease people out of relationships or to make it more possible for them to stay in is another question—and one, essentially, for the couples concerned. But it contains the assumption that conflict is to be expected in good marriages, and that they should not be discarded as "mistakes" because of the differences and disagreements that will arise. In other words, this stance rejects the "commodification" of marriage (if one fails, discard it and select another) in favour of a view of marriage as a potentially therapeutic relationship, one that permits the wear and tear of married life to become a means of personal maturation and social development.

This view might well be criticized for idealizing conflict in marriage and disregarding its potentially destructive effects. And there is no doubt that the therapist's stance will be endowed with different meanings by different people—that, after all, is part of the therapeutic process. Insofar as it is seen to encourage the Platonic view of human nature, one that is essentially unitary, the "meeting and melting into one another" may then be construed as a natural objective in "the desire and pursuit of the whole" What a terrifying prospect for those who yearn to be loved yet are frightened of losing themselves within an intimate relationship; and what an unequally weighted enterprise when women may be more adept than men in carrying out the emotional transactions upon which such a high value is placed. For others, the therapeutic stance may seem to threaten personal security, resembling a potential assault on what Haldane (1991) has described as a primary social system of defence against anxiety, isolation, alienation, loss, and emptiness.

Many couples seeking therapeutic help, and even some of those participating in research interviews, may be unclear about how to define, let alone understand, their experience. Sometimes they will search for an external reference point to answer questions like "Are we normal?" "Do other people you see have this kind of experience?" Therapists, at least, are expected to have answers to questions about what is normal in marriage, and yet, maddeningly to some, they turn them around, insisting that the only viable reference point is personal and particular. The personal and particular then becomes the field for exploring what helps and hinders marriage.

Other cultures see things differently. Speaking in Moscow about connections between public policy and private relationships I put the case, in true western style, for a family policy that enlarged areas of individual choice, promoted tolerance of plurality in family forms, and supported people in discharging the responsibilities that follow from the choices they make. The argument went down like a lead balloon with some people there. In particular, representatives of eastern Muslim countries regarded an extension of the boundaries of individual choice as eroding traditional social and cultural supports. And who is to say they were wrong? The marriage debate takes different forms in different cultures, and it is infused with competing ideologies that support different positions in arriving at a balance between private choice and public commitment.

This links with the second reason for Penny Mansfield's interest in looking at the contributions of sociologists and therapists, and the relationship between them. The two disciplines represent the public and private domains within which couples live out their lives together: marriage is the meeting-point between individual psychology and the study of social systems. Neither private experience nor public context can adequately be understood in isolation from each other. If there are dangers in generalizing from individual experience, there are equal dangers in denying values that do exist and have influence. People cannot develop in a social vacuum; they need to encounter and take account of the realities of others, and in that process they constitute the realities of others.

This is a crucial point, and one that counters the argument that companionship between men and women is a private concern, that it does not impinge on public matters, and that couples should be free to make their own arrangements without reference to anybody else. People who cohabit do not avoid the public concern of the law, nor do cohabitees exclude legal considerations when planning for the future, or when winding up their relationships. The issue is not one of deciding between private relationship and public institution, but of establishing an appropriate balance between the two.

Here is a conundrum similar to the central relationship dilemma in marriage: how to sustain both individual and collective realities. The dilemma is articulated in film and theatre as well as in the abstract of the relationship textbook and the urgent encounters of every-day life. On the one hand there is the tale of Shirley Valentine (Russell, 1988), constricted by the deadening routines of domestic life into a Zombie-like existence (except in the confines of her own head) and brought to life by walking out on her marriage in order to have an affair—not so much with another person or another country as with herself—and risking exposing herself to experiences of which she had previously been frightened. Or there is the dilemma depicted in *Children of a Lesser God* (Medoff, 1982), as a profoundly deaf, non-speaking, yet eloquent woman and her would-be speech therapist and lover struggle with who is to dictate the terms of their relationship: are they to communicate by sign or sound?

On the other hand, and as powerful as the fear of loss of self, is the fear of isolation. Both fears can generate feelings of insecurity, the latter most evident when marriage ends. But the yearning captured in the remnant line of a distant pop song— "I'd rather live with him in his world than live without him in mine"—suggests just how strong the desire to merge can be at the beginning of a relationship.

The problem of me being with you without losing my "me-ness", or you your "you-ness", and the challenge of creating a "we-ness" that constricts neither of us but transcends what we have to offer as individuals is, I suspect, fundamental to any close human relationship. From the "spaces in your togetherness", quoted by Eileen Bertin from Kahlil Gibran's *The Prophet* (1926), and the "distance regulative" functions operating within partnerships, which have been described by Byng-Hall (1986), to the compelling drive for intimacy fuelled by personal need and publicly endorsed as a realizable goal in marriage, there are particular pressures on companionate marriage to manage the tension between aloneness and togetherness—not least when personal identity and satisfaction in life are assumed to derive to such a large degree from it. In these circumstances marriage is both a key part of the personal social environment of couples and a statement of their identity as individuals.

Personal development

Closely allied with companionate values in marriage is the search for personal fulfilment and development. This is articulated in both spiritual and psychological terms, and there is much common ground between the two approaches. Not the least of these similarities is a concern with interpreting experience.

In chapter four, Michael Sadgrove explores the meaning of marriage from images that derive from three sources. The first of these counterposes the two narratives of the creation story as they appear in the Old Testament book of Genesis, followed by the teaching of Jesus in the New Testament. Secondly, there are the marriage rites and ceremonies themselves. Finally, there is the experience that derives from pastoral theology.

The world of theological antiquity restates the historian's premise that nothing is new. The big questions concerning relationships between men and women, human sexuality, different kinds of love, and the meaning of redemption percolate, along with others, through all three sources. Binding them together is the quest for human and spiritual growth through relatedness to others—"person making", as the General Synod report of 1978 put it.

Psychologically speaking, too, marriage has a "person-making" function, and one that I return to in the final chapter of this book. Here, the recreative aspect of the relationship is paramount—both reconstituting past family dramas and creating opportunities to learn through play. The physical and emotional proximity of partners in marriage parallels some of the earliest childhood experiences of caring and being cared for. Marriage actively invites the resurgence of conflicts that remain unresolved from earlier times and of hopes that remain unfulfilled, offering the possibility of reworking issues that hamper development. Viewing marriage as a psychological institution, one that brings his and her inner worlds into conjunction with each other, allowing each to test his or her realities against those of the other, implies, as a matter of necessity if marriage is to be doing its job, that there will be conflict. What, then, distinguishes a marriage that works from one that does not is not conflict itself, but how conflict is managed. Here, one is in the realm of unconscious contracts in marriage—the unwitting selection of a partner because of the potential she or he has for making the self whole. From a theological perspective, Michael Sadgrove describes this as the redemptive property of marriage. Realizing such potential depends on the health of a relationship—a matter that is the subject of chapter eight.

Warren Colman addresses a closely related issue in chapter five. He identifies the principal threat to companionate marriage not as divorce, but as infidelity, and he explores the monogamous ideal as a powerful emotional longing rather than a social imperative. Drawing on literature to illustrate the tension between personal desire and social constraint, he defines fidelity not as adherence to an external code, but as an achievement of moral work that involves renunciation, sacrifice, and tolerance of disillusion. The object of that work—which lies at the heart of psychotherapy—is to bridge the gap between belief and behaviour in a way that is personally integrative and does not leave individuals feeling they are playing the game according to someone else's rules. Development is well removed from the narcissistic pursuit of individualism in this context; it works for both individual and collective interests.

Sexuality

In a wide-ranging review of the social significance of marriage,
White (1992) asserts that societies have always regulated
sexual relationships in one way or another. In the western
world, sexual exclusivity is a hallmark of the ideal traditional
and companionate marriage, and so it acts to regulate sexual
behaviour. Practice does not necessarily conform with intent—
that is one of the destabilizing contradictions in companionate
marriage—but it represents an aspiration shared by couples
and their social community. The wedding ceremony is a public
statement of the transition from sexual availability (sometimes
depicted in the excesses of the stag/hen night) to the sexual
exclusiveness of the marriage bed.

In the past, dual standards of sexuality served to define
women as the property of their husbands. Adultery was a kind
of theft, and before the days of reliable contraception it carried
the risk of introducing uncertainty about legitimacy and en-
titlement for the propertied classes. Even for those less well off,
an economic equation was drawn between sexual pleasure and
financial responsibility. So the premium placed on a woman's
virginity was intricately bound up with her value on the
marriage market—a reminder that the "commodification" of
relationships is certainly not the exclusive preserve of our
present times and that, in aspiration at least, we may be doing
a little better. An Englishman needs time, however. It took until
October 1991 for the Law Lords to overrule Chief Justice Hale's
dictum of 1736 that wives consented to sexual intercourse with
their husbands once and for all when they married. Now the
law of rape operates within marriage as well as outside it.

Sexuality is a powerful symbol, extending beyond the economic domain. Over the centuries it has been represented as a
destructive instinct in men, and, most puzzling, it has been
almost overlooked in women. For women, sexuality has acted
as a symbol of male dominance, so that the increasing likeli-
hood of married women instigating affairs has, in part, been
associated with the processes of female emancipation (see, for
example, Lawson, 1988).

Sexual politics operate within the privacy of marriage as
well as on the public stage; therapists are only too familiar with
the way in which daytime hostility can result in asexuality at

night. The interpenetration of bodies is both exciting and frightening. Remove the fear of pregnancy, and the fear of infection takes over. Overcome the ignorance, guilt, inhibitions and double standards of Victorian sexuality, and there is still AIDS to reckon with. AIDS is a powerful symbol for the fantasy that intimacy with others can result in the loss of self—a kind of death, a fantasy that can excite both recklessness and dread in its promise of fusion.

One feature of companionate values in marriage is the expectation of good sex. Although difficult, it is now possible for men and women to talk together about their sexual relationships. Women are acknowledged as sexual beings. Research into human sexual functioning has reduced ignorance and given rise to new therapies designed to treat sexual difficulties. And, once again, therapists are seen to set, as well as respond to, the marital agenda, constructing expectations and defining problems. What impact does this have on marriage?

In chapter six, Paul Brown traces the development of this new sexual awareness from its mechanistic beginnings to the more rounded appreciation of the differences between men and women and the intercourse they have together. This relational view of sex has implications that extend well beyond the bedroom and implies that the regulation of sexuality has to do with much more than the exchange of bodily fluids. In his metaphor of the ancient charts containing warnings that "there be monsters here", he is concerned only in part with the excited fear that genital sexuality might "rear its ugly head", but more importantly with the apprehension that it may be dangerous to venture into uncharted waters where the wider expression of human sexuality can find expression. The "patient" here is not so much the couple as society's willingness to encourage rather than curb creative relationships between men and women in places that have previously been "no-go" areas for one or other sex.

Children

Traditionally, creativity between men and women in marriage has centred on the act of procreation. Only forty years ago, the Reverend Crowlesmith spoke for many of his generation when he said that marriage should result in parenthood if it were not to be selfish (Crowlesmith, 1951). The great majority of those marrying for the first time today will expect to have children and succeed in so doing. Indeed, a growing proportion of couples starting a family together do not bother to go through the formalities of marriage at all. Why, then, marry to have children?

The nature of public anxiety on this score is most apparent in the divorce debate. In the first place, there is concern about who will pay for children if there is no visible contract between a man and a woman signalling where the responsibility lies. The assumptions here are that men continue to be the main economic providers in families, that they will not have a primary role in child care, and that unless they are "locked in" to their families they will duck their responsibilities. There is some evidence to support these assumptions: only very recently have there been fiscal changes to recognize the separate economic existence of women within marriage; despite growing proportions of married women going out to work, there has been no equivalent increase in men taking on child-care responsibilities; and the Child Support Act, which has recently come into effect in England and Wales, is evidence of a need to create public mechanisms for tracking down errant fathers.

The threat is not diminished by the proposition that women can go out to work and support themselves. While the economy continues to depend on married women and mothers in the workplace (often working part-time and for less than their male counterparts), society depends even more on women to act as carers—usually unpaid, often undervalued, but always relied upon to be there. If women go out to work, who will look after the children? If marriage disappears, who will remember birthdays, organize the relatives at Christmas, and look after granny when she breaks her leg—or granddad when his mental faculties desert him? This is a particularly pressing social question as low birth and death rates swell the ranks of senior citizens. Who will pay for crèche facilities, the care of the infirm and the elderly, and the purchase of housekeeping services? In short, who will society's carers be?

Marriage has served to answer these questions through the institutionalized division of labour between men and women along Tennysonian lines: "Man for the field and woman for the hearth". That distinction is no longer tenable. Despite our egalitarian ideals, we continue, as a society, to elevate the status of earners and diminish that of carers, perpetuating a division of roles along patriarchal lines that limits the choices open to men and women and builds inequality into their relationships. This makes co-operation at home and at work more difficult than it might otherwise be, encouraging competitiveness when one moves into the other's territory, or a polarization of concerns when traditional boundaries are observed. In this light, marriage can be seen as wrestling, relatively unsupported, with a—possibly the—major social issue of the latter half of this century.

Susie Orbach forges a link between the gender issues that are articulated in public debate and what takes place between men and women in the privacy of their own homes. The conscious contract between men who undertake the economic labour and women who carry out the emotional labour is underpinned by unconscious dependency dynamics in their relationships. The consequence of this is that what she terms "women's emotional labour" is rendered invisible. In chapter seven she explores the origins of this arrangement and the psychological investment men and women have in maintaining the status quo.

There is one further point to consider in connection with marriage and children. It has to be asked whether children need two parents to sustain their development. There is no definitive answer to this question, not least because the links between cause and effect are very complex. For example, research indicates that parental conflict is more significant than the events of separation and divorce for the healthy development of children. Conflictful marriage may therefore be as damaging as conflictful divorce. Or again, because the living circumstances of single-parent households are likely to be less advantageous than those of two-parent households, the opportunities open to children may be adversely affected simply through material disadvantage. How can one distinguish between the effects of parenting patterns, secure marriage, and material resources when identifying impacts on children?

From therapist and researcher perspectives, the key issue is less to do with the procreation of children than with their care and upbringing. Three assertions can be made about this: (1) The capacity of people to sustain partnerships in adult life is significantly influenced by the models of partnership they internalize as children. (2) The *quality* of the relationship between parents is an important indicator of how well men and women operate as parents, and this is true whether they are married, living together, or living apart. (3) The attitude and support of the wider community is relevant to the success of the enterprises of both parenting and partnering.

The chapters that follow cross and recross the boundary between individual and collective realities, with the relationship-cum-institution of marriage acting as a filter between the two. The rapid changes affecting relationships between men and women on the socio-economic front affect the personal experiences of those within marriage. The decisions and choices of individual couples similarly affect the social environment of married life. I write this in a year following one in which the third and most celebrated of the royal marriages ended in separation. If the royal family symbolizes all our futures, as Billig (1992) argues, what future is there for marriage? But last year was also one of a royal remarriage, and next year has been designated by the United Nations as the International Year of the Family. What do these contradictory public signals mean? Dr Johnston, no doubt, would conclude that we are caught between hope and experience. In these circumstances, marriage needs to be rethought.

CHAPTER TWO

Learning from divorce

Martin Richards

Introduction

A ll is not well in the state of marriage—or, at least, that seems to be a widespread view. There is much discussion of our "high" divorce rate, the rise of cohabitation, and the number of children born outside marriage, which now approaches a third of all births. It is suggested that marriage is not providing the satisfaction and support it once did. Society seems to have lost its way—that, at least, is the claim. The causes of these changes are usually perceived as a shift in marital behaviour and attitudes and not, for example, as the result of changing economic and social pressures on couples. So it is more likely that the so-called "sexual revolution" of the 1960s will be cited as a cause rather than the present economic recession, with its accompanying housing crisis and high rates of unemployment.

In this chapter I want to stand aside a little from these current debates and draw on the work of social scientists, including historians, to see how far these perspectives may illuminate the current debate. But before doing this, it is worth commenting on what is seen as "the problem".

As with so many public debates about domestic life, the present one talks of marriage and divorce in over-general terms and exaggerates the difficulties. It is widely believed that the divorce rate in the United Kingdom is rapidly rising, whereas, in fact, it has been broadly stable since the mid-1970s (see Elliott, 1991 for a description of recent demographic trends). The rate itself is modest compared with many countries—for example, the United States or any of the Scandinavian countries (here the matter is complicated by very high rates of cohabitation, which are now making marriage a minority status for adults who live as a couple)—and it remains the fact that, on current projections, about two thirds of existing marriages will be ended by the death of one or other spouse. Divorce rates are, in fact, widely variable within the United Kingdom: while those of south east England may be relatively high in the European Community league, Northern Ireland has one of the lowest rates in Europe. I am not suggesting that there have been no changes in the United Kingdom. For instance, cohabitation is now a common phenomenon and is accepted by many in ways in which it certainly was not a generation ago. But while there are significant and important changes, I shall argue that they are, in part at least, the result of long-term processes that have been operating for a century or more, rather than indicating recent sudden change (Richards & Elliott, 1991).

My second point is that not all change is in the same direction. Over the last few decades we have seen a striking rise in what may broadly be called fundamentalism in at least three of the major religions in Britain—Christianity, Islam, and Judaism. These movements have focused on issues related to marriage and family life and are now a potent force, pushing for what they regard as traditional values. Prominent among these are opposition to divorce and cohabitation.

In this chapter I draw on research on divorce and use this as a perspective from which modern marriage may be discussed.

Factors related to divorce

Since the earliest days of marriage research, there has been an interest in divorce. The logic behind the work was straightforward enough. It attempted to isolate factors characterizing marriages that ended in divorce with the idea that these might be used as a basis for intervention—either to head off particularly vulnerable marriages or to provide better help and support for those in trouble. Looking back over what is now more than half a century of such research in North America and Europe, one would have to say, I think, that the results have been rather disappointing.

What this kind of research has succeeded in doing has been to confirm a number of common-sense notions about marriage, but it has provided little by way of understanding. So we know that if spouses are particularly young or old, or the wife is pregnant at her wedding or conceives very soon afterwards, the marriage is more likely to end in divorce, as are marriages where there is a wide gap between spouses, whether this is in age, social background, culture, or religion. Spouses who marry after a relatively brief acquaintance, or who do so against the wishes of their families, are more likely to divorce. Once married, such factors as economic hardship, prolonged absence of a spouse from the house because of work, large numbers of children (or none at all), and, indeed, overt conflict, all show the links with divorce that one might expect (see Raschke, 1987, for a comprehensive summary of this tradition of research). Of course, it may be that this research has simply chosen to look at the more obvious factors and so, not surprisingly, has confirmed what we believed all along. Or perhaps there is little to be learnt at this level of analysis. Maybe once we have dealt with the obvious potential sources of conflict and friction, there is not much more that can be said. It is certainly true that research is now moving away from the demographic level of analysis, and, as illustrated by the other contributors to this volume, there is more of interest to be said about such matters as the beliefs that spouses bring to their marriage and their styles of relating to one another.

My intention here is to develop a rather different perspective, and I want to take the historical correlation between divorce rates and the rise of companionate marriage as the starting point for my argument (Phillips, 1988). What I suggest is that this is not a chance association: companionate marriage is in itself unstable, and it contains the roots of its own destruction. Rather than offering a "haven in a heartless world" (Berger & Kellner, 1964), its apparent safety is an illusion which, for some, will become the bitterness and recriminations of divorce. To simplify an argument that necessarily deals with very complex matters, I will confine my discussion to middle-class marriage in Britain.

Some history

I have argued elsewhere that what has become known as companionate marriage has its origins in the middle-class domestic world that developed during the industrial revolution (Reibstein & Richards, 1992). It is a system of marriage based on individual choice of partner and romantic love, which became well established by the end of the last century. It is a notion of marriage in which the two partners, ideally at least equal in position, set out to share all their domestic life together. Each becomes not only a lover but companion, friend, and confidant, with whom most or all leisure time is spent. However, while this ideal of companionate marriage laid emphasis on the equal and complementary roles of men and women, it developed in a world in which domestic life was widely segregated. While men centred their life in the world of work and politics, women were expected to confine their interests to their homes and a domestic social world. As I shall suggest, the contradiction that this produced remains central in marriage today.

As one might expect in a period of change, issues related to marriage were widely debated in the closing decade of the last century and the first two of the present, leaving a rich source for those interested in the development of modern marriage.

A common line of argument was that the institution of marriage was in itself stifling and antithetical to love. This theme is one that is prominent in the novels of the period—as one fictional character puts it when speaking of love and marriage, why would people want to cook porridge in a Greek vase? A common suggestion was that state and societal control of marriage made it unnecessarily restrictive in ways that damaged the relationship of the spouses. Vera Britten, for example, in *Halcyon or The Future of Monogamy* (1929), argued that more freedom in the form of such things as better sex education, freer access to contraception, and easier divorce for those who made mistakes in their choice of partner would improve marriage, together with improved economic and educational opportunities for women.

Perhaps typical of a slightly earlier period was Maude Churton Braby, who in about 1909 published *Modern Marriage and How to Bear It*. This argues for a marriage based on affection and respect, avoiding passion on the one hand and mere convenience on the other. She suggests that before marriage women need to know something of the world, men, and sex. She extols the virtues of the "preliminary canter" or "ante hymeneal fling" but is quick to point out that women should not sow their "wild oats" quite as literally as men. However, she is not unsympathetic to those who do.

> feminine wild oats, otherwise an ante-hymeneal "fling" . . . a woman—new style—who has knocked about one half of the world and sown a mild crop of the delectable cereal will prove a far better wife, a more cheery friend and faithful comrade. [p. 29]

> a good woman who has surrendered herself to an ardent lover and has been deserted by him must necessarily have gone through such intense suffering that her character is probably deepened thereby and her capacity for love and faithfulness increased. [p. 32]

Within marriage, her expectation is of a continuing double standard. She states that if men are faithful, it is only because of lack of opportunity and disinclination. But however close a friendship and companionship she recommends, she does not believe there should be no secrets in marriage, and she comments that few men are sufficiently "lacking in wisdom to let a wife discover their misconduct". She also addresses the issue of monogamy for women, but in a less direct way through the imagined institution of "duogamy" in which women would have two husbands. Her fictional characters discuss the advantages of this and point out how their interests are much wider than those of men. An obvious interpretation of this would be to see it as a reflection of the way that women were still largely excluded from the male worlds of work and politics and that domestic life represented a larger part of their social world than it did for men.

Important changes took place in middle-class domestic life in the 1920s and 1930s. Servants were now much less common and, if present, were more likely to be a "daily help" than one who lived in. Women undertook more of the domestic work and child care. Inevitably this brought their husbands into closer contact with this work, but there is little indication that they shared in it beyond occasionally helping out at times of crisis. Although a division of labour remained, the social sphere was now a shared one, and this was true both within the home and outside it. I would suggest that an important and growing feature of marriage in this period was the way in which couples spent more time together. Shared leisure activities—involving public entertainment such as the cinema or based on freely available public transport—increased in popularity, and much of this activity would also include the children. This was an era, recorded by many a box Brownie, that established the nuclear family as a social unit.

The Second World War, like the First, led to new attitudes and behaviour in relation to marriage. Women achieved more social and economic freedom, which seemed further to reinforce the idea of marriage as a shared and equal enterprise. The post-war era of prosperity allowed much fuller expression of such ideals. It is often assumed that the 1960s mark some kind of sudden break in marital and sexual relationships. I believe this view to be mistaken, and, as I have argued with my colleague Jane Elliott (Richards & Elliott, 1991), while it may be true that at this time it became possible to speak more freely in public (and probably in private, too) about sexual and relationship matters, changes in conduct were simply the continued development of trends that have a much longer history. The point may be illustrated by changes in the sexual manuals. The old standards, like Van de Valde's *Ideal Marriage: Its Physi-*

ology and Technique (1928), which was first published in 1920, began to disappear. These were books that were explicitly addressed to married couples (although the unmarried were doubtless an important readership) and dealt with sex from an anatomical and mechanical point of view. They assumed men to be initiators but counselled them to be mindful of the needs of their partners. Their replacement titles—for example, Alex Comfort's *The Joy of Sex* (1974), are books of a very different kind, which present diverse sexual activities as pleasure for the mind and body and make no assumptions about the marital status of participants.

Trends that had been growing throughout the century meant that by the 1960s the great majority of couples had experienced sexual intercourse before marriage (Reibstein & Richards, 1992). For most of these, it was no longer restricted to "premarital sex" for a couple who intended to marry, but the experience of a number of sexual relationships in which marriage may not have been part of the agenda for either participant.

Present dilemma

This history, outlined in brief and skeletal form, has left us with a form of marriage that is, I believe, flawed, with deep contradictions that lead to an instability that may be indexed by divorce. It is also reflected in the move by some to replace marriage by cohabitation. But, ironically, the usual forms of cohabitation are based on very similar assumptions to marriage and so lead to the same problems. It is not the marriage vows that cause the problems but our assumptions about marriage and other couple relationships. Love, as writers of popular songs have long recognized, can neither cook meals nor wash clothes, but can it be the central ideology for a satisfactory marriage? Essentially that is the position it has come to occupy in historical middle-class marriage. But I would argue that the difficulties already perceived at the turn of the century in combining love and marriage have only become deeper. It is convenient to discuss these under three headings.

Autonomy and the shared life

Central to the idea of companionate marriage is a shared life. But, as many commentators have described, there is a conflict between the need to construct a relationship based on the notion of a shared life and the desire for individual autonomy, which our modern culture also values highly. Askham (1984), for example, has provided a detailed analysis of the ways in which couples try to find a path between these competing values.

Another way of looking at the same set of issues is to see what happens when couples begin to have children. Though their number may be reduced, having children remains a central priority in modern marriage. Indeed, probably a larger proportion of all women (and, presumably, of men) have children today than in the recent past. Studies of marital satisfaction show that, typically, the high rates found in the first phase of marriage drop sharply as soon as children arrive. The effect is specifically related to the arrival of children and is not simply an effect of the increasing duration of marriage. Why should this be? Why should the achievement of what is still widely regarded as an objective of marriage have this effect? I would suggest three major reasons.

Most women give up paid work when they have children, at least for a time, and they begin to undertake a much greater proportion of the domestic work. The ideal of a shared life, in which both have jobs and domestic work is divided equally between them, can no longer be sustained. The advent of children makes plain the role-segregation and the division of labour for men and women.

The second reason is, of course, that the care of children in our society is both time-consuming and often exhausting. This is well illustrated by the depression that so often is part of our modern institution of motherhood. Parenthood also brings changes in the couples' social world, especially for a mother who may lose the friendships associated with her employment. To some extent this may be compensated for by the development of other social networks, for instance with other women with children and often a reinforcement of relationships with female kin, including their own mother. Despite this, many studies describe an isolated and rather lonely world for mothers of young children.

The third reason I would suggest is that children intrude into the shared and exclusive intimacy that forms part of the ideal of modern marriage. Leisure time—already reduced— has now to incorporate children and their needs. Finding space and time for a couple to be alone together will often involve making complicated arrangements. At a more subtle level, the experiences each bring to their common time may now be more divergent—one from a world of work, the other from nappies and babies. Polly Garter, in Dylan Thomas's (1954) *Under Milk Wood*, might have been speaking of the experience of married motherhood when she said, "nothing grows in my garden, only washing. And babies" (p. 30). This is very different from the romantic and exclusive honeymoon period of a marriage.

Sex before and after marriage

As already mentioned, most people now enter marriage having had experience of earlier sexual relationships. Sex is no longer held to be exclusive to marriage. This, I suggest, means that marriage has to be marked off in other ways from other relationships. This we may see in attitudes towards sexual exclusiveness, which have become more strongly expressed with the growth of the notion of companionate marriage. Even over the last few decades, we may discern a trend towards married people placing a stronger emphasis on monogamy (see Reibstein & Richards, 1992).

We make more fuss over weddings than we used to. Weddings have become more expensive in real terms and are more important socially. It seems we need to mark the change in status more clearly in public and to underline that marriage is something different from the cohabitation(s) that may have preceded it.

But despite the attempts to mark off marriage from other relationships and the emphasis on monogamy, such evidence as we have suggests that over recent decades affairs have become more rather than less common (Reibstein & Richards, 1992). While the double standards of the Victorians may now take rather different forms, the evidence, such as it is (and it is sketchy to say the least), suggests that men are still more likely than women to have affairs.

Several different kinds of factors have probably contributed to the rising number of affairs. Changing patterns of employment, especially for women, and leisure, provide more opportunities for meeting potential extra-marital partners. Easy availability of effective contraception, backed up by abortion, has made the control of fertility more complete outside as well as within marriage. The married, like the unmarried, may share the same assumptions that close affectionate relationships should be sexual and that the expression of sexuality is important to personal development. Having had a number of relationships based on such assumptions before marriage, it may prove difficult, despite intentions of monogamy, to avoid continuing the same patterns after the wedding.

So, at a time when monogamy—for both men and women— is particularly emphasized in marriage, there may be factors that draw the married into other sexual relationships. Ironically enough, the emphasis on sexuality as a central and integral part of any relationship makes an affair more threatening to a marriage than it may have been in the past. Such a shift can be documented in the changing patterns of advice offered in the problem pages of women's magazines. While in the 1950s a wife with an erring husband is advised to be patient and to wait until he comes to his senses, a present-day spouse is much more likely to be told that something is basically wrong with the marital relationship, and urgent action is required (Richards & Elliott, 1991). An added complication is that the nature of affairs may also have changed. Like marriage, the affair may also be companionate, and, of course, a companionate affair always poses the risk that it may become a companionate marriage.

Openness and secrecy

Just as there was wide segregation in the roles of the Victorian middle-class marriage and couples would spend a considerable part of their leisure as well as work time apart, so there was often a degree of formality and distance in their relationship. There was no expectation that all confidences should be shared. Indeed, as can be seen from the marriage manuals of the period and the early decades of this century, the advice was not to share everything. Today the emphasis is very different. Shared confidences are very much a part of what is held to be a good and satisfactory marital relationship. Conversely, a failure to communicate and to share is seen, in itself, to be a marital problem that requires attention. To put it in rather different terms, the pendulum has swung towards a position where the expectation of companionate marriage is that autonomy is reduced and the idea of a merged intimacy is at a premium.

Much can be, and has been, said about exactly where the balance of intimacy and individual autonomy should lie. The point I want to emphasize is the difficulty that the expectation of openness and honesty can create when either spouse becomes involved in other relationships. The evidence suggests that most affairs remain secret. This poses an additional threat as they break the trust of openness on which modern marriage is based. As the authors of a book on American marriage comment, "marriage makes couples more deceptive" (Blumstein & Schwartz, 1983). For those who work therapeutically with couples, there are obvious problems that arise in connection with the ways in which marital secrets are dealt with.

Conclusions

In this chapter I have tried to suggest that the evolution of modern marriage is such that it contains some fundamental contradictions. Necessarily, the argument has been very condensed, and it has not been possible to do full justice either to the historical material or to the complexities of modern marriage. In particular, I have discussed marriage in broad terms and have not fully reflected its variety, the very different experience of men and women and of those in varying social and economic circumstances. However, the broad sweep does have the advantage of focusing attention on issues that will arise for all couples.

Of course, marriages are dynamic relationships that change over time. Each spouse brings a series of beliefs and expectations about marriage to their relationship, and together they begin to construct a shared reality in the light of those beliefs and those held by members of their social world (Berger & Kellner, 1964). The process of construction will be influenced in many ways by their social and economic position. In the course of the development of their relationship they must find resolutions for the contradictions that I have outlined. Many couples, of course, do this successfully—successfully in the sense that they find a way of conducting their relationship that is more or less satisfactory for both of them. Others do not, and seek alternative partners or other patterns of relationship. We need to continue to analyse the formation and dissolution of marital relationships and the social context within which this occurs, so that we may become more realistic about one of the most central of our social institutions.

CHAPTER THREE

Public perceptions: private experiences

Penny Mansfield

The title of this chapter mirrors a typical contrast: public set against private. There are other means of expressing it—for example: outer world–inner world, social–psychological. All too often when marriage is discussed it is the point and counterpoint that are stressed. Therapist and sociologist stand on either side of marriage, one inside, one outside, each tending to view the other's perspective predominantly as a backdrop to their own observations.

However, a growing number of sociologists and therapists working in the field of marriage and family relationships yearn for a greater dialogue, each recognizing the value of widening their observations—that private lives have public significance, and, correlatively, that social trends have individual consequences (Collard & Mansfield, 1991). Marriage is, then, "a bridge between public and private worlds" (Clulow & Mattinson, 1989). Indeed, the family can be regarded as the

The author wishes to acknowledge the considerable contribution of her colleague, Jean Collard, to the issues explored in this chapter.

unique nexus of the individual and society, combining and reflecting both the structural and the personal at one and the same time.

From a temporal dimension also, family experience is one of constant oscillation and containment, holding within it the impact of the past, the present, and the future. Our sense of history and of the future are inextricably bound up with the complex web of relationships that have composed, and that currently compose, our "family". All of which is more simply and elegantly expressed by Shils (1981), when he writes:

> The first link in the chain which builds past and present and future into the structure of a society is reforged every time an infant is born and survives. [p. 169]

Although the examination and understanding of process is of central concern to therapist and sociologist alike, they frequently regard each other's perspective as a static context against which experience takes place and not as an integral part of that experience. This chapter focuses on neither the public nor the private, but on the interconnection between the two, exploring the flow and interrelationship between them, which illuminates the continuities and interactions between individual experience and the broader context of social structure. It sets out to do no more than provoke further reflection on the way in which public perception constitutes personal experience and vice versa. Reciprocal processes such as these are difficult to analyse, which is perhaps one reason why we so often resort merely to identifying and describing the polarities.

Professional enquiry and image-making

For the past decade I have been involved in a longitudinal study of the early years of marriage. After publication of the first book from the study (Mansfield & Collard, 1988), I received many invitations to address a wide range of groups—from sixth formers to family-planning nurses. One of the groups I addressed was a branch of The National Housewives' Register (a national organization set up to provide a discussion forum for women who are based at home, caring for families). My brief was to provide a portrait of contemporary marriage, and I was careful to preface my talk with details of methodology: to explain that this was *a* portrait, not *the* portrait of marriage. Afterwards I resisted several attempts by members of the audience to regard me as a marriage "expert"; however, I realized later that by disseminating findings from a research study on marriage, I was contributing to a public perception of marriage.

The main focus of my talk was on gender. Through the words of the husbands and wives we had interviewed, I presented evidence of *her* and *his* marriage. In particular, I highlighted the discrepancy between egalitarian attitudes to marital roles and the day-to-day reality of "who does what in the home", and the very different meanings that the word "togetherness" held for the spouses in the research study. Husbands were seeking a "*life in common*" with their wives: a home life, a physical and psychological base, somewhere and someone to set out from and to return to. But for nearly all the wives the desired marriage was a "*common life*", with an empathetic partner who was to provide both material and emotional security. These wives sought a close exchange of intimacy in which they would feel valued as a person and not just as a wife.

My talk sparked a lively discussion. Many women spoke personally of their own marriages, their experiences resonating with the accounts of the women in our study. From my point of view it was encouraging to have the research findings validated by another group of wives. As I was leaving, one woman, who had not spoken at all during the evening, approached me. At first her manner was diffident, but she then enthusiastically thanked me for "saving my marriage"—a common response for therapists, perhaps, but not one sociologists are used to. Rather nervously, I asked her to elaborate. Married for 12 years, she had, she said, "a marriage that appears to work—from the outside looking in". However, over the years she had felt that something was missing, and this missing element was "closeness". Her husband never communicated his feelings to her, and he seemed awkward, even mystified, when she disclosed her own feelings to him. "To begin with I thought there was something wrong with me. Then I thought there was something wrong with him; and lately I have been coming to the conclusion that he does it deliberately to annoy me. But after your talk I realize he is like most men, can't help it really. Knowing that's what marriage is like—not just my marriage— will help to make it work."

This woman's reaction stirred an uncomfortable feeling in me. She had received from me something I was unaware of giving—a definition of marriage. Not a prescriptive definition. Not an ideal model of marriage. Quite simply, she had used the account of what a group of other peoples' marriages were like to locate *her* marriage. She was suggesting that, for her, marriage "worked" if it was statistically the norm—that is, like most other marriages. Her expectations of closeness were not being met, but as long as most other wives were similarly disappointed, her disappointment was bearable; and if her husband was no worse than other husbands, then she would not torment herself with the belief that he was doing it on purpose. Of course I do not know whether by reviewing her expectations in the light of my talk her marriage did, indeed, "work", but her response to my talk set me thinking further about how those of us who report on marriage, as researchers and as therapists, contribute to the expectations of married people—how as observers of and commentators on a variety of private experiences of marriage we create public perceptions of marriage.

Our experiences of interviewing newly-wed couples made us aware of the subtle ways in which we, as interviewers, both consciously and unwittingly purveyed implicit definitions and assumptions about marriage. All the couples who took part were traced through the marriage notices; a few men and women asked suspiciously, "why us?", but to most people it seemed an unremarkable request. However, when we started to discuss the form of the interview, several men and women challenged our request to interview them and their spouses separately. For some it seemed unnecessary. So sure were they that their answers would be the same they could not understand why we should put ourselves to the trouble of asking questions twice. For the rest, our motive was sinister—an unwelcome bias on our part towards seeing them as two separate individuals rather than as a pair, for we were suggesting that each spouse had *different* things to say in answer to the same question.

And, of course, we were. A primary objective of our enquiry into contemporary marriage was to explore gender differences in marriage and to consider the tension between the pursuit of individual identity and becoming a couple. To explain this to the men and women we were about to interview would have involved a discussion of marriage; instead, we deflected the challenge by pointing out that the first part of the interview consisted of questions about their *individual* pasts, and that it would save time to do this separately. The fact that questions about their marriage followed on was overlooked once interviewing was under way. However, at certain points in the interview, particularly in the section on domestic activities, many respondents betrayed their curiosity, anxiety even, about what their spouse might be saying in answer to the same question. Presenting themselves as a couple meant playing down, in some cases even denying, any differences between them. At the time the interviews took place, there was a television game show called *Mr and Mrs* in which spouses were separately asked identical questions about each other's likes and dislikes. The "ideal" Mr and Mrs (for whom there was a prize) were the couple who "knew" each other so well that their answers were the same—a public presentation of marriage as uniformity that was beamed into many homes. No wonder that several respondents expected our interview to be imitative of the television format . . . with similar assessment criteria for establishing which were "good" marriages.

Another aim of our enquiry was to examine the nature of marital equality. Did the couples want equality? What did they mean by the term? How, in practice, was this construed in their marriages? A criticism of several studies of the domestic division of labour has been that the questions asked have frequently been based on the assumption that there are specific roles for husbands and wives, and that these are allocated according to traditional divisions of men's jobs and women's jobs in the home. To avoid this, we took the view that in every household there is a set of basic domestic tasks that have to be regularly undertaken. Each partner was then asked who had most recently performed any of these tasks in their home. In the vast majority of marriages wives carried the "lion's share" of the domestic chores, even though they were usually working similar hours outside the home as their husbands. For many men the net effect of having to answer repeatedly "she does it" produced uncomfortable feelings. They became defensive, as if the interviewer had actually challenged their lack of involvement, and these men offered unsolicited justifications for their lack of participation in daily domestic activities. The framework of the interview had made them aware that they did not practice what they said they believed. Some husbands may have been left with the impression that the interview was designed to do just this; that it was part of our purpose to promote an egalitarian model of marriage.

Any study of marriage conducted at a time when it is supposed to be changing is likely to appear to be offering a model of marriage founded upon new orthodoxies. To ask questions, however neutrally, about "other ways" easily implies support for those "other ways". At the time of the interview with the newly-weds (1979), it was usual for women to give up or change their employment in some way when they became mothers. This practice was being challenged, and, indeed, legislative changes a few years earlier had paved the way for new mothers to remain in paid employment. We sought a form of questioning that could be used with women *and* men—one that did not assume that when children arrived it was the mother who gave up work. So when discussing employment each respondent was asked, "Do you think there will be a time when you cease work for a while?" For wives there was an obvious answer: "when I have a baby" was the common reply. For husbands this was a strange enquiry. Many sought further clarification: "do you mean redundancy, the sack?" Their responses demonstrated that traditional values prevailed—strongly. Asking such a "strange" question had lingering effects in some interviews; for the first time, the interviewer intruded—she was not "one of us".

Among the husbands and wives we interviewed, the common view of marriage was of a relationship founded upon emotional satisfaction, yet their reasons for getting married belied a strong investment in the institution. All marriages were different, there were no rules, and yet there was a fascination with other marriages and how their own marriage stood in relation to these. Some yearned for confirmation that theirs

was "a proper marriage", and by "proper" they meant normal—
that is, like other marriages. For a small minority there was a
desire to demonstrate that their marriage was most definitely
not the norm. In light of the fact that they had recently committed themselves to a permanent and exclusive relationship it
was not surprising to find that all were keen to gauge whether
their marriage was "working" relative to some external standard, to which we, as marriage observers, were deemed to have
access. Throughout the interviews there were rhetorical statements, such as, "I expect you find most young couples are the
same?" . . . "I suppose she's like most wives in that respect?"
. . . "I don't suppose our difficulties are any greater than anyone else's?" After the interviews had finished, the interviewers
invariably stayed for refreshments and a chat with the couple.
Once again there were rhetorical questions, but also more
direct enquiries about the other couples. These conversations
revealed that we were regarded as marriage experts not because we knew a lot about marriage *per se*, but because we had
detailed knowledge of so many other marriages.

Marriage:
institution and relationship

In considering the complex interplay between changes in
marriage, in marital agencies, and in society as a whole, David
Morgan (1992) comments that:

> it is often maintained that marriage has become more of a
> "private" relationship; indeed this is part of the distinction
> between institution and relationship. There are, however,
> some paradoxes within this formulation. Most striking, as
> has already been noticed, is that this "private" relationship
> has become more and more the focus of public discourses.
> [p. 27]

If one over-arching theme emerges from the wide variety of
writings on the nature of change in marriage, it is that marital
change can be described in terms of a move from institution to
relationship. The change of name of the "National Marriage

Guidance Council" to "Relate" strikingly exemplifies this. The distinction emerges originally in the middle of this century in the writings of Burgess and Locke (1945), who described a move from "institution" to "companionship" marriage. It has become widely accepted that over the centuries men and women have moved away from marriage as a legal bonding founded upon social and economic considerations to an emotional bonding, "the marital relationship" founded exclusively on love and the pursuit of happiness. Such an account can be found in counselling textbooks, public documents, "self-help" guides, and even in the narratives of ordinary husbands and wives describing their attitudes to and experiences of marriage. However, the notion that, in the past, the relationship between husband and wife was entirely focused on and constrained by their publicly defined roles is as misleading as to assume that in modern times men and women conduct their married lives solely in terms of an intimate personal relationship. The concept of marriage as a social and economic unit *and* as an intimate relationship is ever-present: it is the emphasis in public perception of one concept over the other that decides which is to be preferred and thus taken as typical of a particular era.

Some contemporary writers on marriage consider the concentration on marriage as a means of personal fulfilment as overly exclusive:

> Marriage as a practical social enterprise seems an almost forgotten topic, so involved have we become in "relationships". . . . Is the future likely to be a return to a far more practical and down-to-earth institution with a new balance of roles but more related to the way in which marriage was seen in previous times? [Green, 1984, pp. 302–303]

For others, the shift in emphasis is a rejection of the institution, based on an interpretation of institution as a combination of the formal conscriptions of State, Church, and, of course, Law. Scruton (1986) states that people who marry:

> pass together into a condition that is not of their own devising. . . . The obligations are not contracted between partners but imposed by the institution. [p. 356]

From this perspective, modern lovers wishing to carve out their own individual roles as partners will reject such an imposition and repudiate a model of marriage as essentially the performance of roles, of having obligations, duties, and correlative rights, all of which have been carefully defined. However, this is a notion of institution as some fixed entity, which lies outside human agency. The implication then drawn from rising divorce and increasing cohabitation is that the institution has been rejected in favour of the relationship.

A regular question in Gallup Polls asks, "Is marriage an outdated institution?" One wonders what most of those polled understand by the concept of marriage as an institution. As a sociologist working with counsellors and therapists, I have been aware that, to the non-sociologist, a sociological approach to marriage is one in which the structural aspects of marriage and family life are over-emphasized, at the expense of the relational. Such a view may stem from the 1950s and 1960s, when sociology had achieved a new popularity. Family sociology was then heavily influenced by the functionalist perspective, which directs attention to the macro-social context rather than to the interaction between individuals, placing emphasis on the functions that marriage fulfils, both for the married couple and for society. However, there are other sociological understandings of the term "institution", ones that recognize the dependence of institutions on human agency. Giddens (1981) argues that an institution can exist only if people attach legitimacy to its prescriptions and proscriptions:

> by institutions I mean structured social practices that have broad spatial and temporal extension . . . and which are followed or acknowledged by the majority of members of society. [p. 164]

While cultural patterns endure, they change over time. Institutions are not handed down as tablets from on high but are created by men and women who both conform to them and, in turn, change them. At any period one can detect both institutional and relational aspects of marriage; and within any period there is likely to be variation according to class, religion, and ethnic group. Over the life of an individual marriage there will be variation too. The relational aspects of marriage may be pronounced when the couple are newly-weds, institutional aspects highlighted when children are born, and then another relational form appearing when children have left home. In discussing the impact of social change on contemporary marriage, Kiely (1984) talks of a continuum from companionship marriage to institutional marriage that applies to contemporary marriage rather than marriage viewed historically. It is a point echoed by Handy (1990), in his book, *The Age of Unreason*, when he describes "portfolio marriages" as a form of serial monogamy where the marriage changes without changing partners:

> Marriages have always needed to adjust to the stages of life, through child-rearing, to adolescence, to the empty nest and retirement. The new requirements of the workplace, the move towards more portfolio lives, more paid work for qualified women, more work from home and more telecommuting, the increase in earlier retirement, second careers and Third Age re-thinks, these all have their impact on the marriage. If the relationship does not flex in some way it will break. Too often, serial monogamy or a change of partner is the way many people match their need for a marriage with a need for change. [pp. 154–155]

In his major study, *Modernity and Self-Identity*, Anthony Giddens (1991) argues that modern institutions differ from all preceding forms of social order:

> in respect of their dynamism, the degree to which they undercut traditional habits and customs, and their global impact. However, these are not extensional transformations: modernity radically alters the nature of day-to-day social life and affects the most personal aspects of our experience. Modernity must be understood on an institutional level; yet the transmutations introduced by modern institutions interlace in a direct way with individual life and therefore with the self. [p. 1]

Giddens uses the term "modernity" to refer generally to the industrialized world, and he identifies *reflexivity* as one of three major influences on the dynamism of modern institutions. The social sciences are, he argues, inherent elements of the institutional reflexivity of modernity, and he refers extensively to a variety of manuals, guides, self-help books, academic studies, and therapeutic texts as "not just works 'about' social processes, but materials which in some part constitute them":

Personal problems, personal trials and crises, personal relationships: what can they tell us, and what do they express, about major changes in the external social environment of the individual, affecting marriage and the family as well as other institutions; yet people carry on their personal lives much as they always did, coping as best they can with the social transformations around them. Or do they? For social circumstance are not separate from personal life, nor are they just an external environment to them. In struggling with intimate problems, individuals help actively to reconstruct the universe of social activity around them. [p. 12]

Taking as a specific example the investigation of divorce and remarriage by Wallerstein and Blakeslee in *Second Chances* (1989), Giddens points out that although this is a work of sociology, it will have a readership comprising counsellors, social workers, and ordinary men and women who have been divorced:

Second Chances is one small contribution to a vast and more or less continuous outpouring of writings, technical and more popular, on the subject of marriage and intimate relationships. Such writings are part of the *reflexivity* of modernity: they serve routinely to organise and alter the aspects of social life they report on or analyse. [p. 14]

Marriage in present times is undergoing a transition. There is a move away from marriage in the sense of kinship and obligation, to another form of close relationship, which is socially recognized and fortified. A reconstruction of "marriage" appears to be underway:

I think people will probably continue to get married for some time to come but also that "marriage" will gradually imply something quite different. Having no major implications for affinal relations, for descent, for future marriages, for the transmission of social identity from one generation to another, it will be primarily a public affirmation of the couple's identity and fortification of the fact that two people are a couple. Though not marriage in a kinship sense, it will by no means be meaningless. [Corbin, 1978, p. 208]

Each and every couple, in varying ways, is caught in this act of reconstruction. Counsellors have tended to focus on marital problems and to locate these problems predominantly in the personalities of the spouses (Kiely, 1984). A more realistic contemporary perspective is to consider *marriage as a problem* rather than *marital problems*. In our interviews with newly-wed couples we found that men and women shifted between different and, at times, even contradictory images of marriage. Public images of marriage are confused and confusing, and the world of private example is equally perplexing and paradoxical. Spouses are constantly seeking clues about marriage and about other people's marriages because they want to make sense of their own. What to do? How to act? Who to be? According to Giddens these are focal questions for everyone living in circumstances of late modernity. There are echoes of this in a survey by Davis and Murch (1988) of men and women who had divorced when they suggest that many people may be using the legal system to find out whether their marriage is at an end.

Researchers and therapists are also caught up in this act of reconstructing marriage. Morgan (1992) has examined the relationship between the changing construction of the problem of marriage and divorce and the changing approaches of the marital agencies in a case study of Relate, and he concludes that:

> marital agencies do not simply respond to individual troubles or social problems but do, in an important sense, constitute these problems and troubles. These reciprocal processes, whereby practitioners respond to the "needs" of individuals with troubled marriages while simultaneously constituting these needs, represent one of the main bridges between institution, marriage and society. [p. 33]

In rethinking marriage, social researchers and therapists alike need to be continuously aware of how they create frames of reference, how they define, both explicitly and implicitly, what "works" and what does not. We do not stand on either side of marriage; rather, we occupy the same space, somewhere between public perception and private experience.

CHAPTER FOUR

Theological images of marriage

Michael Sadgrove

I t is perhaps not usual to find a theological paper in company such as this. But as the poet quoted at the outset of Maggie Scarf's book, *Intimate Partners*, puts it, "[in] every house of marriage there's room for an interpreter" (Scarf, 1987, p. 7). A theologian is an interpreter of the stories people tell. He or she interprets those stories from the particular vantage point of belonging to a faith-community. Theologians can collaborate with interpreters from other disciplines in helping to draw the contemporary "map" of marriage. Perhaps it is the particular contribution of theology to draw attention to the "why" questions alongside the "how": if marriages are to work, it is important to ask why marriage exists, what it is *for*. That is the aim of this chapter.

It is worth making three points at the outset. (1) A very significant number of marriage ceremonies in Britain still take place in church, over half of them in the Church of England. No doubt, there are many reasons for getting married in church, not all of them consciously religious. But many couples would seem, in some way, still to want to place their marriages in the religious sphere, where language about God will be used to give

51

meaning to marriage in general, and to their own marriages in particular. And that is to find ourselves already in the arena of theology. (2) Whether we like it or not, our western understanding of marriage has been almost entirely shaped by Christian theology. That legacy is still with us, even if the evidence is that it is breaking down. Since many of the couples who come for marital counselling or therapy will, consciously or unconsciously, have inherited this cultural understanding of marriage, it is important for professionals in other disciplines to know what in fact it is, even if it is only to challenge or reject it. (3) I want to allay any fear that when a theologian starts talking about marriage, what he or she is *really* interested in is divorce. It is true that some kinds of theology seem obsessed with questions of marital discipline and what the Church should do about it. But that is not the primary concern of this chapter.

How, then, are we to arrive at a theological meaning for marriage? What are our sources to be? If we are to paint anything like a complete picture of marriage, three sources require attention. First of all, and most obviously, we need to listen to what the Christian tradition has to say about marriage. We need, that is, to hear the past that has so powerfully formed our image of marriage in western society: the Scriptures of the Old and New Testaments, and the way they have been interpreted through the centuries. (In this chapter, I restrict myself to the Judaeo-Christian tradition as it has shaped our theological understanding of marriage in the west. Of course, in the multi-cultural society of today, theology must be given a wider definition; but that would extend the scope of this chapter.) To listen to the past is not necessarily to become stuck in it. It is simply to overhear those of earlier ages wrestling with the questions we wrestle with now, and to appreciate that even then those questions rarely permitted simple answers. But more than this, to listen to the past prevents us from thinking that our own contemporary age has an absolute monopoly of rightness. To see ourselves in the light of history can help to place our insights and achievements in a larger context.

Secondly, we need to listen to the marriage rites and ceremonies themselves. How we ritualize life-events is a statement of how we understand them. This applies particularly to the marriage service in church, which is so rich in theological images. Many people, asked what they thought "the Church" believed about marriage, would turn to the marriage service, where the aims and ideals of marriage are spelt out. But although they are not discussed here, "secular" ceremonies should not be excluded from the process of theological reflection. They, too, derived largely as they are from the western Christian liturgical tradition, contain similarly significant theological material.

Finally, we need to listen to our own human experience. Professionally speaking, this includes what we call *pastoral theology* reflecting on pastoral process in the light of religious faith. In the sphere of marriage, this will mean the pastoral care of a couple preparing for marriage, or the care of those whose marriages are in trouble. This is the place, familiar to all parish clergy, where theology and praxis, tradition and human experience, interact and frequently collide. The meeting of professional disciplines in this pastoral task is itself a source for theology. Christian pastoral theology has much to learn as it reflects on the insights of the other caring professions. But pastoral theology is more than that which arises out of professional care. We need also to listen to the stories of men and women who fall in love, marry, survive marriage, fail to survive it, fall out of love, separate, divorce, marry again. We need, that is, to listen to our own stories. In this, as in all human experience, we find the raw material of theology as we ask where meaning is to be found in the world as we experience it.

My approach is to explore the theology of marriage primarily through the stories and metaphors that are found in the Bible, looking first at the Old Testament and then at the teaching of Jesus. This is not to make any claim as to their *authority*. It is simply to use the texts that are familiar to many of us, and that in any case lie at the heart of the understanding of marriage in the west. But I aim to do more than merely expound texts. I want to engage in conversation *with* the texts, both by drawing out *their* questions to us, and also by articulating some of the contemporary concerns that arise out of our own experience, whether as professionals with insights from the human sciences or simply as living, loving, feeling human beings with our own stories to tell.

Marriage as an image of God

For Jewish and Christian believers, the exploration of marriage begins with the Book of Genesis. There, in the poetic language of the creation stories, is given an account of marriage that has always been fundamental to Jews and Christians alike. There are two narratives of creation: an earlier one, that of Adam and Eve in the garden of Eden, dating from around the tenth century BC, and a subsequent one, depicting the six days of creation, from perhaps five hundred years later. (These dates refer to the *written* texts we have in the Bible. No doubt the underlying oral traditions are very much older.) In some ways, the stories are in tension with one another. For instance, the earlier account has the man created first, with the other living things (including the woman) created round him and for him, while in the later one, humankind, male and female, is the climax of the entire process. So already, we hear the biblical text in dialogue with itself, and over an issue very much our own in contemporary debate—namely, the roles of women and men, and the placing of humanity in relation to the world.

> So God created humankind in his image, in the image of God he created them; male and female he created them. God blessed them and God said to them, "Be fruitful and multiply, and fill the earth and subdue it: and have dominion over the fish of the sea and over the birds of the air and over every living thing that moves upon the earth." [Genesis 1:27,28][1]

Humanity is created in (or, perhaps better, as) the "image" of God, a visible, tangible icon of what God is understood to be like. The text appears to relate this directly to two things: the differentiation between male and female, and the responsibility put on the human beings for the world. Theologically, these belong together. The male–female differentiation, Genesis suggests, which we can take to mean our human capacity for affective relationship, is what marks us out from the rest of creation. Genesis 1 is very concerned to place everything correctly on the map of creation: light and dark, inanimate and animate, plants, birds, animals, "each according to its kind" is the recurring phrase. The identifying feature of humanity, it says, is that we can know what it is to enter into relationship, consciously to love, and to be loved. But—and this is where the other side of being in the divine image comes in—all this is to be lived out responsibly, in the light of our capacity to make choices, to respect the claims of others and of the environment in which we are placed. The vision of Genesis is of humanity behaving creatively and not destructively, as befits the species ennobled with this profound and mysterious role to be the bearer of the Creator's image in creation.

Later Christian reflection fills out this picture of male and female created in the image of God. It suggests that what is true for human beings—that we can make and sustain relationships—must therefore be true in some ultimate sense of God as well. In other words, God can be understood as being, in essence, relationship, affect, love. That most elusive Christian claim, that God is Trinity, is perhaps fundamentally about loving relatedness. Father, Son, Holy Spirit: what holds this divine threefoldness together is love, for "God is love", says the New Testament (1 John 4: 8). In other words, what is imaged in humanity is this essential nature of God, that God is all love— love between the persons of the Godhead, love flowing out from the Godhead into all creation. It is very striking that when the early Christians attempted to find a Greek word that would do justice to love as they had experienced it in Jesus, not one of the existing, commonly used terms would do. ερως was perceived as specifically sexual and obsessive in its connotations; φιλια, "friendship", not passionate enough; στοργη, "affection", too general. So they rescued from oblivion an obscure word, αγαπη, and invested it with rich dimensions of theological meaning. It came to stand for that noble, committed, self-giving love-to-the-end that they saw in Jesus. From him, they concluded that αγαπη must describe how God so loved the world (Lewis, 1960; Nygren, 1932). Theologically, then, the relationship of marriage, if it is truly love, is agapaistic as well as erotic. It shares in the divine nature. We might say, somewhat rhetorically, that we see in marriage an image of God, reflecting a divine inner life.

It is worth noticing at this point that the Genesis story has profound implications for the way we talk about God. It is significant that it is humanity as *male–female* that is said to be in the image of God, not the male only. This is surely all the mandate we need for recovering and applying female language and imagery in our God-talk, and redressing the imbalance present in what to many is perceived to be the oppressively male-dominated nature of classical theology. It is a curious fact that the language that speaks of God as Mother, while owing so much to the Bible and certain spiritual writers of the middle ages, arouses such passions in many worshippers, as if it is something essentially new-fangled and feminist-inspired (Furlong, 1984; Hampson, 1990; Holloway, 1991; Stein & Moore, 1987).

But there is another implication here. The male and the female are ordered to "be fruitful and multiply and fill the earth". This seems to say that love between men and women is in its very nature *procreative*—that is, acting as a creative, life-giving, energizing force on behalf of God the Creator. Genesis identifies this procreative aspect of marriage with childbearing, and one of the major ethical debates within Christianity has been whether a marriage contracted without the will to beget children is valid.

Perhaps this technicality misses the point of the Genesis text. For its insight is that love between persons is not closed in upon itself. On the contrary, love seeks to transcend itself, find new ways of giving, create space for others. The act of creation, as Genesis tells the story, can be understood as God "stepping back" to allow space for other lives to come into being. Divine love, says the tradition, is open in character, hospitable, inclusive; this is precisely why it is truly creative. There is a fruitfulness of marriage that is more than childbearing. We all know of childless marriages that have a wholeness about them, a creative goodness that is a thing of beauty. So, fruitfulness is to do with quality of relationship, with human and spiritual *growth*, with fulfilling our God-given potential. We could say, in the words of a Church of England report, that a good marriage is "person making" (General Synod, 1978)—biologically where that is desired and possible but, more important, humanly. The opposite is that destructive state of being closed in upon oneself, absorbed with oneself to the exclusion of other lives, what theologians call *sin*. No doubt our professional work brings us into contact with marriages that have that quality about them too.

There is another refrain in this hymn-like story of creation: "and God saw that it was good". The words occur at the end of each day's creative work. At the climax of the whole process, on the sixth and last day, the refrain is reinforced "and God saw everything that he had made, and indeed, it was very good" (Genesis 1: 31). Clearly, this "very good" means, amongst other things, the sexuality of the newly created human beings. I should not have to underline this, were it not for the well-known reluctance of Christian thought to celebrate the goodness of sex. Medieval theologians, following Augustine, saw all human sexual acts, even within marriage, as flawed by concupiscence—a view that has proved enormously influential in Christian history (Brown, 1988). The attitude known as "Manichaean", that sees the material order as a dangerous, subversive threat to the spiritual, has been endemic in Christianity since early times. Paradoxically, it is precisely the *Christian* faith that proclaims a God who has become flesh and committed himself to the material order. There is a contradiction here between a world-affirming, incarnational *theory* and, historically at least, a world-denying, pessimistic *practice*. There should be no doubt that Christianity powerfully reinforces the celebratory world-view of Genesis, not least its joyous embracing of sex and human love.

To see this, it is worth comparing the prefaces to the marriage service in the *Book of Common Prayer* (1662) and *The Alternative Service Book* (1980). The 1662 book sets out the reasons for which marriage exists as follows:

First, it was ordained for the procreation of children, to be brought up in the fear and nurture of the Lord, and to the praise of his holy name.

Secondly, it was ordained for a remedy against sin, and to avoid fornication; that such persons as have not the gift of continency might marry, and keep themselves undefiled members of Christ's body.

Thirdly, it was ordained for the mutual society, help and comfort that the one ought to have of the other, both in prosperity and adversity.

By 1980, they read:

> Marriage is given, that husband and wife may comfort and
> help each other, living faithfully together in need and in
> plenty, in sorrow and in joy. It is given, that with delight
> and tenderness they may know each other in love, and
> through their bodily union, may strengthen the union of
> their hearts and lives. It is given that they may have
> children and be blessed in caring for them. . . .

There is a very significant shift of emphasis here. Not only
is childbearing relegated from top of the list to bottom and
marriage now seen first and foremost in "companionate" terms,
but also the understanding of sex within marriage is trans-
formed from a grudging acknowledgement that marriage is a
"container" to avoid sin, to a much more positive (if still slightly
coy) recognition that sexual joy is one of the supreme gifts of
marriage. In this respect, the Church is some way ahead of the
register office: secular ceremonies tend not to mention this
central sexual fact of marriage. Are our registrars more ill at
ease with sexuality than the Church?

But there is an opposite mistake to make, that of reducing
human sexual relations to a set of techniques, the performance
of which is a matter of skills only, and not of love. Not all
manuals on sex therapy wholly avoid stripping sexuality of its
mysterious, almost sacred, character. Paradoxically, this, of
course, is the precise objection to pornography: not that it
celebrates sexuality, but that, by robbing it of its ecstasy, it in
fact reduces it to a mechanism. The vision of sexual love in
Genesis is, by contrast, bound up with what Albert Schweitzer
calls "reverence for life". The mediaeval woman–mystic writer
Julian of Norwich talks about "courtesy" to living things. This is
what lies behind the traditional Christian sexual disciplines:
that sexuality requires the committed relationship in order to
release its ecstatic, we may even say mystic, dimension. Eros
must walk hand in hand with Agape: selfless love be inflamed
by passionate desire for union with the other; yet that very
God-given desire must itself be redeemed by putting the other
first. That is what it means to be an embodied human being.
That is what "incarnation" means.

Marriage as paradise

I have taken the later creation story in Genesis first because, as we have inherited the shape of the Bible, it is the one that provides the context in which we read the second, older account in the second chapter of Genesis. So, what does the story that follows add to what we have already explored?

Straight away we find ourselves in a different atmosphere. Gone is the cosmic sweep of the story in Genesis 1. We have left behind the sonorous, liturgical rhythms and cadences; now we enter the more primitive world of myth. Here, everything is more intimate, more winsomely naive. Into the garden of Eden, God puts the man he has formed. There, Adam (whose name in Hebrew simply means "humankind") faces his condition, his solitariness: "it is not good that the man should be alone". So God creates the animals and sets Adam to name them, "but for the man there was not found a helper as his partner"; so the woman is formed out of the man's side. Then Adam recognizes that here is what he has been longing for:

> This at last is bone of my bones and flesh of my flesh; this one shall be called Woman, for out of Man this one was taken, Therefore a man leaves his father and his mother and clings to his wife, and they become one flesh. And the man and his wife were both naked, and were not ashamed.
> [Genesis 2:23–25]

An implicit subordination of woman to man is undeniable here, however beneficently intended. This is in sharp contrast to the equality of the man and the woman in the first story. But this should not prevent us from seeing, in this picture, some telling insights. First of all, it is important to note that this is unambiguously a text about marriage. This is not so clearly the case with Genesis 1, however much we tend to *read* it that way. That celebration of male and female in the image of God refers simply to all sexual relationships between women and men, and their procreative outcome. Marriage is not actually mentioned, though it is probably implied. Here, by contrast, the story is told as a way of *explaining* the institution of marriage: "therefore a man leaves his father and his mother". Marriage, in other words, is rooted in the paradisal beginnings of human history. From creation, this was the will of God for humanity. Marriage, says the story, is more than a regulation of sexual relationships in society, and more than society's provision for a context within which children may be brought up. It is grounded in the created order itself. It has a cosmic dimension.

The theological point here is that, as a Church of England report on marriage discipline pointed out twenty years ago, there is "no such entity as *Christian* marriage, except in the sense of the marriage of Christian men and women" (Archbishop's Commission, 1971, p. 14). Marriage does not belong to the Church (or to any other body, even the State), because it is part of the natural order of things. Neither the Church nor the State can technically *marry* anyone. Only individual human beings can marry one another: they are the true celebrants of the rite. Church and State may (and do) *regulate* marriage. Christians may *interpret* marriage in distinctive ways, apply to marriage ideals and principles that derive from their particular faith, as may Muslims and Hindus and Sikhs. But the institution itself belongs to humanity. That is why the Church of England's historic position has unambiguously been that it has the duty of solemnizing the first marriage of any parishioner, whether a baptised Christian or not, for whom there are no legal impediments. For the same reason, the Church of England recognizes the full validity of marriages contracted in register offices. There is nothing second-best about such marriages. All belong to humanity, and, therefore, theologically speaking, all belong to God.

This is perhaps the place to say something about the continuing popularity of Church marriages. It is very striking, at least in my own experience as a parish priest, that most of those who seek a Church wedding are not themselves active churchgoers, nor, often, are their parents. So, what is it that draws them? Undeniably, the setting of a parish church, the structure of the rite, the resonances of the words of the liturgy, all contribute to a sense of occasion that is perceived not always to be present at the register office. No doubt social custom, particularly in rural areas, plays a part, although decreasingly. What we see here is what sociologists call "implicit religion" or, more commonly, "folk religion". This is the innate, largely unexpressed religious instinct that comes to the surface at the major times of passage: childbirth, marriage, death. These are precisely the times when we should expect that there will be those who look for some sense of patterning and connection in life. This is what the Church's rites of passage provide (Carr, 1985; Van Gennep, 1960). It is not to disparage religion to say that it functions as a "container" during periods of major transition. Theologically, this folk-religious instinct appears to be an inchoate acknowledgement that the fundamental moments of the human story point to the mystery at the heart of life. They connect it to the cosmos, to destiny, to God. Marriage, says Genesis, is like that. It is "a great mystery" (Ephesians 5: 32).

We cannot help being struck by another feature of this primitive story. It is the motif of *aloneness*. First, Adam is alone in the garden, and God makes a companion for him. But even then the couple remain alone, in their Arcadia, surrounded by plants and animals, neither possessing nor needing any other human society. Even God, it seems, discreetly conceals himself, so that Adam and Eve may be unintruded-upon in their intimacy, alone in their new-made world. There is a deep psychological insight here. On their wedding day, a couple find themselves, in a way that is both wonderful and terrifying, *alone* with one another: naked, exposed in every sense, unprotected, and totally present to another human being. By that very token, they are distanced from even the closest representatives of the human race: "A man leaves his father and his mother and clings to his wife, and they become one flesh". (It is worth noting the force of the Hebrew word here: he clings to her, almost, we might think, for protection; for he is as much tied to her as once he was one flesh, umbilically, oedipally even, with his mother. Unconsciously, Genesis recognizes an archetypal human theme.) This aloneness-as-a-couple is dramatically ritualized in the marriage service. After the priest has pronounced the couple to be husband and wife, they at once leave their families and kindred behind and follow the priest to the altar, where they kneel alone. I have noticed that, for some brides' and bridegrooms' mothers, this is the psychological moment of leave-taking when the tears flow; for now, irrevocably (as the service assumes), son and daughter have separated from father and mother and are alone in the world, with only each other to turn to. In some marriages this alone-ness is too much to contemplate. It can become loneliness, a kind of death.

Marriage, then, according to Genesis 2, enables a woman and a man to find the completion of their selves in one another: "this at last is bone of my bones, and flesh of my flesh!" Relationship is fundamental to human life. A man or woman is not merely impoverished, but in a profound way *disabled*, incomplete, where there is no "Thou" to respond to the "I" (Buber, 1959), where everything and everyone else is no more than an "it". This is not to say that marriage is, or ever can be, a self-sufficient state of affairs. As the biblical story continues, Adam and Eve find that their aloneness takes on a new dimen-sion: it is not absolute, but is placed in the context of a new society, their own offspring. Once more, love is generous, pro-creative. But this relational "I and Thou" element in the Genesis myth does suggest that, theologically as well as psychologically, marriage makes whole; it heals. It enables me to become more the man or woman I have the potential of becoming. "Bone of my bones, and flesh of my flesh!" is picturesque language to describe that "unconscious wisdom" well known to marital therapists, whereby men and women very consistently recog-nize and choose, as their life partner, precisely that person with whom he or she will come to grow and achieve individuation. Theologically, that process is called redemption. Significantly, it is just this image of redemption that a New Testament writer chooses to illuminate his discussion of marriage:

> Husbands, love your wives, just as Christ loved the church and gave himself up for her . . . so as to present the church to himself in splendour . . . so that she may be holy and without blemish. In the same way, husbands should love their wives as they do their own bodies. [Ephesians 5: 25–28]

The author, writing out of a patriarchal environment, does not draw the conclusion that this redemptive quality of love might be something *mutual.* But we can read the text recipro-cally and see in it an apt insight into the healing nature of a good—or "good-enough"—marriage.

We may say, then, again a trifle rhetorically, that the Adam and Eve myth presents marriage as a return to Eden. A couple's joy in each other, and its healing, redemptive qualities, make for paradise restored. There is a strong element of *play* in marriage, not least in the sexual play of a husband and wife as naked as if back in Eden, innocent as children, celebrating the sacredness not only of sex, but of laughter, happiness, and fun (Berne, 1973). Redemption has sometimes been seen as the power of dance, playfulness, and song to heal the world. Catholic theologians speak of marriage as a *sacrament* (Dominian, 1981, p. 256): an "outward and visible sign of an inward and spiritual grace", as the *Book of Common Prayer* defines sacrament. In the case of marriage, a theologian wants to say, there is a true and effective participating in the healing, redemptive, life-giving, even playful love of God. "In this encounter between husband and wife there is the meeting point between a man and a woman who every moment of their lives, face, react and respond to the presence of Christ in each other" (Dominian, 1967, p. 222). Whether or not the couple see their marriage in consciously religious terms is not the point. What matters is that marriage is intended to be, for all human beings, a charism, a grace-gift. The words Jung had inscribed above the front door of his Zurich home are apt here: *Vocatus atque non vocatus deus adest:* "whether called upon or not, the Deity is always present" (Van der Post, 1976, p. 155).

Marriage and the kingdom of God

So far, I have attempted to outline how theology understands the institution of marriage. It reflects the image of God; and it recreates paradise. It is procreative, person-making, and healing. With the rest of creation, it is profoundly *good*.

At the same time, we can see how the classical theology of marriage has built into it at least one disquieting element: the subordination of woman to man that is very marked in the earlier Genesis story. As we turn to the next phase of that story, we find this even more strongly underlined through the part the woman is said to have played in that disruption of human innocence that we call the fall. On that account, the aetiological story imposes on womankind two penalties: her pain in childbearing, and her subjection to her husband, who, the text says, shall "rule" over her (Genesis 3, *passim*).

We can see a principle at work here which has proved crucial to the way in which marriage has been understood until the present century. It is that marriage has become a hierarchy, in which the husband "owns" his wife as his property (Countryman, 1989). There is nothing unique in this: the ancient world universally understood marriage as a contract that upheld a husband's position in society and enabled his clan to be preserved through the production of legitimate offspring. Thus the law of marriage in the Old Testament provides, for example, for a husband to divorce his wife "because he finds something objectionable about her" (Deuteronomy 24: 1)—that is, a man may dispose of his wife as if she were his property. No similar provision is made for the wife. She is no longer her own. Indeed, a woman in ancient society could in only a limited sense ever regard herself as an autonomous, self-determining individual. She began life as the property of her father; she became the property of her husband. Adultery, therefore, is not primarily an offence against moral purity, or loyalty, though that element is certainly present. Rather, it is an offence against *property*, that is to say, a particularly serious kind of *theft*. It is striking that in the Ten Commandments, the prohibitions "you shall not commit adultery" and "you shall not steal" are found next to each other (Exodus 20: 14, 15).

We grasp the importance of this as we turn to the New Testament and the teaching of Jesus. It is necessary to point out that his teaching about marriage is almost wholly occasional—that is, arising out of particular questions put to him, or situations to which he responded. As we should expect, those questions and situations tend to be problem-centred, addressing, for example, the issues of adultery, divorce, and remarriage. I think we can assume that, in central respects, Jesus would have understood marriage in its "creation" sense, as I have outlined it from Genesis. Indeed, he is recorded as quoting from both Genesis stories in this key text from the gospel of Mark, which is generally regarded as being earliest in date:

Some Pharisees came, and to test him they asked. "Is it lawful for a man to divorce his wife?" He answered them, "What did Moses command you?" They said, "Moses allowed a man to write a certificate of dismissal and to divorce her." But Jesus said to them, "Because of your hardness of heart he wrote this commandment for you. But from the beginning of creation, "God made them male and female." "For this reason a man shall leave his father and mother and be joined to his wife, and the two shall become one flesh." So they are no longer two, but one flesh. Therefore, what God has joined together, let no one separate. . . . Whoever divorces his wife and marries another commits adultery against her; and if she divorces her husband and marries another, she commits adultery. [Mark 10:2–12]

We see at once that this is a radical departure from the marriage legislation of Israel. For it provides for the wife to divorce her husband: that is, *he* is regarded by Jesus as *her* property, just as much as *she* is traditionally *his*. At a stroke, then, Jesus reinstates the equality of female and male within the marriage relationship. This daring claim is at one with what we know from elsewhere in the gospels of his treatment of women, to whom he accorded both a status and a nobility far above the norm in a patriarchal society. Hierarchy between men and women, specifically, but not only, within marriage, is abolished. "In Christ there is no male and female" writes St Paul (Galatians, 3: 28). There are to be no more gender distinctions between human beings, any more than there are to be distinctions based on race ("Jew or Greek") or status ("slave or free"). There is only one, new, humanity, in which all are equal before God.

This radical overturning of the traditional theology of marriage is one that our society, and the Church in particular, is assimilating only very painfully. There is a deep patriarchal dis-ease with what women are seen, subliminally, to represent: untamed sexuality, the impurity of menstrual blood, the mess of childbirth. It manifests itself in the Church by arguments against the ordination of women to the priesthood and by the exaltation of female virginity (Furlong, 1984; Hayter, 1987). In marriage, the traditional gender-stereotyped roles of wife and husband are still uncritically assumed by many married couples from their wedding day onwards. (The new Anglican rite of marriage attempts not to collude with this. The provision for a bride to promise to "obey" her husband is no more than an option, in my experience little used. The patriarchal "giving away" of the bride is likewise optional. The service makes the attempt to depict marriage as an equal, symmetrical partnership between human beings, symbolized, for example, by the identical form of the marriage vows, and the permitted mutual giving and receiving of rings—Stevenson, 1982.)

Jesus' account of marriage is novel in another respect: his prohibition of divorce and remarriage. His saying in Mark's Gospel is absolute: no exceptions are allowed. The logic is based on the Genesis theology: marriage brings a man and a woman into a unique relationship of mutual belonging: "they are no longer two, but one flesh", "joined together" says Jesus, "by God". On this is based the marriage discipline of the western Church, that marriage is a lifelong union that only the death of one of the partners can end. In Matthew's account, an exceptive clause is introduced: "Whoever divorces his wife, *except for unchastity*, and marries another commits adultery" (Matthew 19: 9). Probably, this refers to the Old Testament provision for divorce, where, as we have seen, if a husband finds something displeasing in his wife, he may divorce her. This "something displeasing" was taken by one school of more liberal rabbis to mean a wide range of failings, some very trivial, like overcooking her husband's meal; the stricter school confined it to sexual impropriety only. It is clear that Jesus sides with the more rigorous interpretation; moreover, the text very possibly refers *not* to acts of marital infidelity committed by the wife after marriage, but to her husband discovering, on the wedding night, that she was not in fact a virgin in the first place.

Why should Jesus have taken such a strict view of divorce and remarriage? Theologically, we have seen that mutual loyalty and commitment is an implication of the Genesis theology of "one flesh". But we need to understand the wider context of Jesus' message. He comes, say the gospels, to preach the kingdom of God, by which he means the sudden, decisive breaking into the affairs of this world by God's sovereign rule. We can, I think, safely say that he believed this event to be imminent and cataclysmic, marking the end of the present world order. The whole tenor of his teaching is, therefore, to summon men and women to prepare for what is at hand and reorientate their lives accordingly. The Lord's Prayer is a good example of this kind of theology: "your kingdom come, your will be done on earth as in heaven" (Matthew 6: 10).

According to Jesus, the kingdom's imminent coming makes everything else provisional, not least institutions like the State, Marriage, and the Family. Jesus himself seems not to have been greatly interested in any of these institutions. With the end of history at hand, all that mattered was the coming crisis. So, we can hear him say, this is no time for people to be contemplating rearranging their marital affairs. The time is coming when marital status will count for nothing. For the present, even marriage and the family are more about becoming than arriving: they are to serve the future, not the present. To divorce and remarry would not only amount to a falling-short of the kingdom's demands, it would be to fiddle while the world burns. We find just the same end-of-the-age thinking in St Paul, where the coming crisis is seen as a reason for remaining in the condition the believer found himself or herself at baptism, be it married or single. In this context, it is interesting to speculate about whether times of national or international crisis in history have a *stabilizing* influence on marriage and the family, or a *destabilizing* one. Clearly, the New Testament plea for upholding the marital *status quo* was contending, in some places at least, with an equally persuasive ethic that took as its slogan: "let us eat and drink, for tomorrow we die" (1 Corinthians 15: 32).

This apocalyptic message is a long way from our own understanding of history, even in a nuclear age. The problem for us is that, alien though it is, this is the setting of Jesus' teaching. We tend to hear his words *simpliciter*, as if they were addressed to twentieth-century human beings, without regard to the enormous change of context that has taken place over the intervening period. The all-important *hermeneutic* task of *interpreting* an ancient text in a modern context is too easily forgotten. So a traditional theology of marriage reads out of the text a discipline that is assumed to be normative for all time, rather than seeing it to have been formulated in a period of great turbulence, with a powerful belief that the existing world order would soon be toppled for ever.

Where, then, does that leave the teaching of Jesus as far as our theology of marriage is concerned? We can say four things:

- Jesus endorsed the Genesis stories and affirmed the God-givenness and goodness both of marriage and human sexuality.
- He believed that a man and a woman were equal partners in marriage, each belonging to the other.
- He believed that *in principle* the union of a man and a woman in marriage was a union of lifelong loyalty and love.
- *But* he believed that even marriage was provisional, subject to the higher values and concerns that he called the kingdom of God.

More than this we cannot read directly out of the words ascribed to Jesus. I have already said that his teaching on marriage is unsystematic, *ad hominem.* But we can, I am sure, go further by looking at his way of dealing with those who, in their own eyes or the eyes of others, had failed, fallen short in some way of his, or their, exacting standards for marriage. It is abundantly clear from the gospels that Jesus was a man of the utmost compassion. The woman caught in the act of adultery records a classic conflict between what the religious leaders *expected* him to do (endorse the death penalty by stoning) and what he actually *did* (invite whoever was blameless to throw the first stone and then to pronounce the woman forgiven): "Neither do I condemn you: go your way, and from now on do not sin again" (John 8: 2–11). It is a truism to say that for Jesus sexual offences were by no means the worst a person could commit against God or neighbour, although continuing, bad-tempered debates about sexuality in the Church might suggest otherwise. But, equally, the teaching of Jesus is not libertine or amoral. "Go and sin no more" is a mandate to live more responsibly as a sexual human being, honouring the sexual property of others, and having regard to the consequences for others and for ourselves of our sexual behaviour.

There is, then, an undeniable tension between the "one-flesh" Genesis theology that Jesus affirms and reinforces and his treatment of those who fall short of it. The Church's marriage discipline needs to take proper account of both. Theology is, after all, not only something taught but also something *lived*. The example of Jesus is as theological as his words, and by our own acts we, too, demonstrate where our theological priorities really lie. It is not part of my task to show how the compassionate treatment of the divorced, including the celebration of subsequent marriages in Church, might work out in practice, although the evidence is that in the Church of England, at least, an increasing number of clergy appear willing to celebrate second or subsequent marriages in church. It is enough to say that it must be an urgent priority for the Church to come to a common mind about its practice in this difficult area if it is not to become very quickly out of touch with the contemporary realities of marriage and divorce in our society.

Conclusion

I have tried to trace a theology of marriage as it seems to me to emerge out of the Old and New Testament, and to which, perhaps without realizing it, we are, for all our modernity, still in debt. The Jewish and Christian traditions offer insights, glimpses, that may help us understand what is demanded of us, whether as people who are married, or as those helping others to find more meaning and happiness in marriage. But there are also elements in the tradition towards which we need to be questioning and critical. Theology is not about finding formulae. It is more a process of identifying questions, and then pondering those questions in the light of faith. Sometimes that involves theologians in considerable struggle. Arriving at a theology of marriage adequate to the needs of the present day is no easy task.

70   MICHAEL SADGROVE

In so far as all of life is a gift from God, then marriages are, surely, "made in heaven". In so far as all of life is our human responsibility, then marriage is one of life's most demanding, yet rewarding, tasks. Rethinking marriage, to make it work, is very much both God's work and our own.

NOTE

1. Biblical quotations are taken from the *New Revised Standard Version* of the Bible (Oxford University Press, 1989).

CHAPTER FIVE

Fidelity as a moral achievement

Warren Colman

I t is a curious fact that while attitudes towards pre-marital
sex and divorce have become far more liberal over the
past fifty years or so, attitudes towards extra-marital sex
have, if anything, hardened. While most people now accept that
marriage will not be the only sexual relationship they have in
their lives, and even that the marital relationship itself may not
last for ever, around 90% still appear to believe that marriage,
at least while it lasts, should be sexually exclusive. One may
have more than one partner, but not more than one at a time.
Strictures against infidelity may therefore be considered as the
last bastion of the monogamous ideal.

Yet it is an even more curious fact that these attitudes are
not at all matched by behaviour. The taboo against infidelity is
one more honoured in the breach than the observance. It is, of
course, notoriously difficult to acquire reliable statistics on a
matter of this sort, not least when it is still the subject of
considerable moral disapproval. Nevertheless, research evidence indicates that a reasonable, and probably conservative,
guess would be that some infidelity takes place in around half
of all married couples (Lawson, 1988). This is certainly the case

amongst those couples coming to the Tavistock Institute of
Marital Studies, where an affair is by far the most common
presenting problem, often being the precipitating factor that
leads couples who have been unhappy for some time to seek
help (Clulow, 1984).

Why, then, does the taboo remain? In chapter two, Martin
Richards suggests that in an era of companionate marriage—or
at least an *expectation* of companionate marriage—the quality
of the relationship becomes the main binding force of marriage;
extra-marital relationships therefore threaten the fabric of
marriage more than they would where marriage is defined in
more strictly socio-legal terms as an institution.

This shift in the definition of marriage is part of a much
larger social process associated with secularization and plural-
ism. Moral questions can no longer be decided purely by
reference to an externally given set of rules imposed by Church
and State but have become increasingly a matter of individual
choice and circumstances. Although it is arguable whether the
Church ever held sway over the beliefs—let alone the actions—
of the entire population, it certainly had a much more central
role in defining dominant moral expectations in the past than it
does today. Christianity has, in fact, been the main factor in
defining the monogamous ideal as the yardstick against which
we are now measuring moral and social change. When marriage
as an institution was primarily wedded to the Church—and for
some, of course, it still is—it was more than a social institution:
it was also, potentially at least, a spiritual one. For those who
believe, the Church's sanctions are more powerful than those of
society: sexual fidelity is maintained not only in relation to the
marital institution, but to the religious one as well. The sinner
betrays not only their spouse but their religion. There is, therefore, the possibility of exclusion from a spiritual community as
well as from a personal relationship.

The point is that what may have happened for many people
is a shift in the *location* of moral concerns. In a pluralistic and
secular society the idea of sinning against God's law becomes,
for many, an insubstantial and possibly meaningless abstrac-
tion. Instead, there is an increasing concern with individual
and personal relationships. That is, extra-marital relationships

are now seen as threatening the marital relationship, whereas in the past they were seen as threatening society and betraying God. The moral code has become personalized. To have strayed no longer means having deserted the flock of God the shepherd, it means having been sexually unfaithful to one's human spouse.

Despite these changes, and despite the fact that other incursions into the monogamous ideal are now tolerated, this particular incursion is still regarded as unacceptable. Why should this be? This question does, I believe, turn on the tensions inherent in marriage between institution and relationship. Whereas in the past the relationship was defined in terms of the institution, now it is the other way round. That is, being legally married is no longer definitive of the relationship between the partners. Marital therapists frequently ask the question, "Is there really a marriage here?"—meaning, "Is the quality of the relationship sufficient to consider the partners to be *psychologically* married?"

In these terms marriage is a personal reality that may or may not correspond to the socio-legal one. It is not only the location of the sanctions that has changed, but the definition of marriage itself. To the extent that marriage is regarded as a personal matter, it is up to the couple to say when they are married and when they are not and, therefore, when the rules of fidelity are intended to apply. And because expectations of fidelity remain a defining feature of almost all marriages, extra-marital sex continues to threaten it *as an ideal* in a way that even divorce does not. Although many marriages survive affairs, those that wish to hang on to the monogamous ideal in spite of them do so with some difficulty. For the rest, it is my view that the relationship suffers, and the balance is likely to shift towards the institutional aspect of the relationship and away from personal intimacy.

Paradoxically, then, the increased acceptance of pre-marital sex and divorce serves only to accentuate the need for fidelity within marriage. Since neither sexual relationship nor legal marriage defines marriage-as-a-relationship, fidelity has become the touchstone of what does. But if fidelity remains so important, as apparently it does, why is there such a gap between aspiration and reality? Why, when disapproval of infidelity is so great, do people continue to have affairs, and possibly even more so than before?

This question can be turned on its head to ask why some people do *not* have affairs, and why so many of those that do apparently retain a belief in fidelity. For infidelity is only problematic in the context of a continuing belief in fidelity.

Fidelity and the monogamous ideal

This belief is not a new thing—indeed, it is very old, at least as old as the Book of Genesis, where Adam says about the creation of Eve: "therefore shall a man leave his father and mother and cleave with his wife and they shall be one flesh" (Genesis 2: 24). The implication that "one flesh" is exclusive is made explicit in the seventh commandment: "Thou shalt not commit adultery."

Furthermore, although monogamy is not universal, marriage in one form or another is. It is the most basic form of social relationship and therefore constitutes a fundamental building block of social structure. This is especially apparent in tribal societies, as numerous anthropological studies demonstrate. Kinship structures are very diverse and often very complex, but all contain rules about marriage. Regulation of sexual and procreative relationships is an essential feature of any society whose structure is founded on kinship, and sanctions against adultery make obvious sense when seen in this light.

It is important here to distinguish between monogamy and fidelity. Those who believe that everyone else should believe and act as they do—and this belief is written into the evangelical mission of Christianity—tend to judge others according to their own lights and hence regard anything that does not conform to the monogamous ideal as adultery. The Mormons of Utah have suffered appallingly in this respect—persecuted and ostracized for the best part of a century because of their preference for polygamy. It is therefore very interesting to note that a modern polygamous family in Utah (who are not Mormons) maintains a belief in fidelity. Alex Joseph, who has nine wives (a number of others have not stayed the course), explained to Oprah Winfrey on her television show that he never has sex with anyone who is not his wife, and his wives, who all seemed remarkably content with the arrangement, each maintain a monogamous relationship with him. The point here is that sexual fidelity constitutes the boundary around an agreed set of relationships. Transgressions of that boundary tend to inspire guilt in the perpetrator and condemnation and wrath in others, but how the boundary is defined may vary from one culture to another.

A further important distinction is between the monogamous ideal and the pursuit of an ideal relationship, although these two issues are frequently confused. The monogamous ideal refers to a capacity to sustain a relationship even when it is not ideal. The Christian marriage service, with its references to "for better, for worse, for richer, for poorer, in sickness and in health", makes this clear enough. The psychological relationship to this ideal is brought out more clearly by the term "infidelity" than by "adultery", although in their essential meaning they are clearly linked. "Infidelity" means a lack of faith and belief; it is linked to the word "infidel", which brings out its connections with religious faith. Applied to marriage, it means a failure to keep faith with the marriage contract, a falling-away from the ideal, which inspires guilt and shame to the extent that belief in the ideal is retained.

In clinical work with couples, I find that guilt about affairs is pretty much universal, although it does not always surface for some time. Curiously, it is often the betrayed partner who feels shame and humiliation, perhaps because it is they who are still faithful, not only to their partner but to the ideal of an exclusive sexual partnership; the infidelity is felt to have besmirched that ideal. This, of course, is the link with the term, "adultery", meaning "to adulterate, contaminate, and defile".

For couples who engage in marital therapy, the wish to achieve a monogamous relationship also seems to be universal, despite the prevalence of infidelity. I have never seen, or even heard of, a couple whose stated goal at the beginning—let alone at the end—of therapy was to be helped to manage infidelity. Although many couples are helped to loosen an over-rigid bond that limits autonomy, this never seems to include permission to have affairs. This may be because the bias of the therapists influences the clients, although I doubt this, since in many cases marital therapists regard an affair as an attempt to make a more satisfying relationship. Clinical evidence supports Annette Lawson's sociological findings that adultery brings many people to life and can be used as a means of self-development, although not necessarily in the way she suggests (Lawson, 1988).

Another reason for the monogamous tendency of couples in therapy is more difficult to refute: namely, that they are a self-selected sample. For example, it may be that those who wish to pursue non-monogamous relationships do not turn for help to an Institute of Marital Studies. It is possible that those who work in other settings have a different experience.

I have therefore turned to literature and film, rather than clinical case material, to illustrate and develop my argument. Although these choices are also self-selected, they have the advantage of enduring appeal to far more people than ever see the inside of a psychotherapist's consulting room (or are included in a sociologist's research questionnaire, for that matter). In my view, psychotherapy is closer to literature than it is to social science, since novelists, dramatists, and poets are similarly concerned with the minutiae of individual motivation and feeling. Works of art are both the expression of psychic reality and a means of giving that reality specific form. When they are popular, as all the examples I will be referring to are, they clearly speak to the psychological and social condition of many, and when they are lasting, they clearly transcend particular historical moments.

Moral work in marriage

Before considering the literary illustrations, I wish to make a further point, which leads towards a definition of the monogamous ideal and also indicates why it is so rarely achieved. Although it is felt as a need, it cannot be actualized, except through considerable *moral work*. This does not, of course,

mean the rigid adherence to an externally given moral code—
that is an avoidance of moral work just as much as the
complete abrogation of any morality. What I have in mind
includes the psychotherapeutic goal of making the unconscious conscious, but I deliberately use a more traditional
terminology to indicate that the goal of psychotherapy is itself a
modern version of a much older problem—namely, what constitutes a "good life", or, in terms that reveal the coalescence of
moral concerns and the medical model, "the wish to get better".

In relation to marriage, "getting better" requires the reconciliation of personal and social needs. This is, of course, a
central dynamic in the personal aspects of couple relationships—the tension between the needs of the individual and
those of the partnership. Askham (1984) described this as the
conflict between identity and stability, but this is in some ways
a false dichotomy since stability is an essential prerequisite of
identity. Another way of looking at it might be to see the tension
as being between stability and flexibility, or order and change,
which can degenerate into a polarized opposition between rigid-
ity and chaos. These tensions are not only worked out *within*
marriage, since marriage as a social institution stands at the
cusp of the tension between individual and society, the private
and the public. Therefore the nature of marriage itself reflects
this tension in society at large, and the way that individuals
relate to marriage indicates their response to this universal
dilemma. Issues like this do not have ready-made solutions,
and it is the struggle to arrive at a satisfactory resolution of the
conflict that I describe as moral work. Obviously, infidelity
focuses this tension in a particularly acute way, but I would
(first) like to illustrate it by reference to a novel that is not
concerned with infidelity at all but does have a great deal to say
about the need to find a resolution between personal inclination and social conformity: Jane Austen's *Pride and Prejudice*.

Subsequently, I shall compare Jane Austen's portrayal of
the making of an ideal marriage with two classic stories of
infidelity: the film *Brief Encounter*, written by Noel Coward, in
which fidelity eventually wins the day, and Flaubert's *Madame
Bovary*, in which infidelity ultimately fails to release the heroine from the trap of an inadequate marriage. I will also refer to

Hardy's *Jude the Obscure*, to underline how different from, and even contradictory to, an externally imposed morality is the notion of fidelity as a moral *achievement*.

Pride and Prejudice

The central theme of *Pride and Prejudice* is the growth of an unlikely relationship between the proud, haughty, and reserved Darcy and the lively and playful Elizabeth, who is initially prejudiced against him. It is apparently a classic love story, with a happy-ever-after ending. Despite living in a highly structured society, which requires strict obedience to its rules of propriety, Darcy's love for Elizabeth overcomes his disapproval of her unsatisfactory social position. As Tanner (1972) puts it, "one of the gratifications of the book is that Elizabeth and Darcy seem to demonstrate that it is still possible for individuals to make new connections in defiance of society".

At one level, the novel therefore looks like an early exposition of the supposedly modern idea of romantic marriage—marriage entered into by the free choice of the partners on the basis of romantic love. It certainly does show that the idea of companionate marriage dates back at least to the beginning of the nineteenth century (*Pride and Prejudice* was published in 1813).

Consider the following passage, when Elizabeth, having previously rejected Darcy's proposal, has realized her error.

> She now began to comprehend . . . that he was exactly the man who, in disposition and talents, would most suit her. His understanding and temper, though unlike her own, would have answered all her wishes. It was a union that must have been to the advantage of both; by her ease and liveliness, his mind might have been so formed, his manners improved; and from his judgement, information and knowledge of the world, she must have received benefit of great importance. But no such happy marriage could now teach the admiring multitude what connubial felicity really was. [p. 325]

But to regard Jane Austen's vision of connubial felicity as no more than an expression of the modern ideal of romantic love would be to fail to grasp the subtle complexity of her understanding of right relations between individual and society. For the modern view of romantic love regards right relations as a purely personal matter. Social constraints are seen as undesirable obstacles that can and should be overcome. In the tension between marriage-as-relationship and marriage-as-institution, the focus is almost entirely on the relationship, the institution being regarded as an irrelevant encumbrance. Many couples do not even enter into legal marriage, or do so purely for practical reasons, such as financial considerations. Even those who criticize the romantic ideal of marriage by contrasting it with its often prosaic reality are suffused with an ideological bias towards purely personal relationships, in as much as their critiques often betray a barely disguised disillusionment with the marital institution.

This is not Jane Austen's position at all. She does not present the relationship between Darcy and Elizabeth as in opposition to social mores, but as a transcendence of them, a demonstration of their true intention. Elizabeth's unsatisfactory social position is contrasted with her superior character, to show that the true embodiment of the social ideal is not a matter of class or social connections at all, but a matter of individual sensibility and, above all, a moral consciousness.

Austen portrays a social world that is at once the real world full of recognizably flawed human beings and at the same time an ideal world in which all such human limitations are transcended via the aesthetic harmony of her artistic vision. She is, in this respect, like a literary version of Mozart and, like him, represents the last glittering beauty of the Enlightenment before the darker passion of Romanticism began to take hold of European cultural consciousness.

It is Romanticism that gives voice to the demand of individuals to pursue their own destiny regardless of social constraints, which are regarded as artificial obstacles. Where the Romantics stress passion, excess, and the free play of the imagination, the eighteenth-century classicists stressed reason, moderation, and the requirements of propriety. Jane Austen's achievement, standing at the cusp of this cultural change, was to portray a vision in which the demands of individual *and* society could be reconciled. Marriage should be neither merely institution, nor merely relationship, but a reconciliation of both in which reason and emotion, Darcy's regulation and Elizabeth's lively playfulness, each have their place and are balanced by the other.

Austen uses the conventions of the romantic novel to create something altogether more muscular and challenging. In her novels, marriage does not simply happen as a consequence of love, nor are the impediments to it only of an external nature. On the contrary, love only develops as the consequence of *a change in consciousness* in one or more of the central characters. Elizabeth, for example, comes to recognize that what she took to be her accurate discernment of Darcy's character was merely prejudice.

> Had I been in love I could not have been more wretchedly blind. But vanity, not love has been my folly. . . . I have courted prepossession and ignorance and driven reason away, where either were concerned. Till this moment I never knew myself. [pp. 236–237]

The ideal marriage requires self-knowledge based on reason as well as love, and, perhaps, as a central component of love. Yet equally it requires the engagement of hearts and minds, and not merely obedience to social conventions.

These issues are illustrated by the counterpoint provided by two other marriages that take place in the course of *Pride and Prejudice*. The first is between Elizabeth's friend Charlotte and Mr Collins, a pompous and ingratiating clergyman who judges everyone according to their social position. Theirs is a marriage of convenience in which romance plays no part whatever. Each marries the other as a socially suitable partner in order to maintain and possibly enhance their social position.

Charlotte's choice is an entirely calculating one, based on the economic necessities of her social position. Elizabeth understands but cannot share her attitude—she has already rejected Mr Collins. For Mr Collins, however, she displays only contempt and ridicule—men, at least, have more opportunities for free choice. Here the institution of marriage has entirely eclipsed the possibilities of relationship.

The second marriage is between Elizabeth's younger sister, Lydia, and the soldier, Wickham. Theirs is a marriage based entirely on emotion. Lydia is swept away by her immature romantic ideas and persuaded into an elopement, which can only result in social catastrophe. As Tanner points out, in the terms of the novel "passion is hardly differentiated from folly. Lydia's elopement is seen as thoughtless, foolish and selfish, rather than a grande passion" (p. 38). This marriage is the opposite of the earlier one and shows how far Jane Austen is from espousing the modern ideal of romantic love. Sexual love is regarded as a wholly inadequate basis for marriage.

The fundamental issue here is the relationship between the individual and the social order. The individual pursuit of satisfaction regardless of social consequences—and here I am thinking of infidelity as well as Lydia's elopement—is disruptive of social order and stability but stresses values that are crushed by a too-rigid adherence to what the social order prescribes. How can the competing claims of personal needs, which are disruptive of social order, be reconciled with social needs, which are restrictive of personal satisfaction? In the real world there is always a tension between the two, but in the world of the novel the ideal marriage is contracted not only between the two individuals, but between the themes and issues inherent in the novel itself. Thus, individual and society are shown to be part and parcel of one another. The route followed by Lydia results in personal impoverishment just as much as the route followed by Charlotte. The individual needs the social fabric within which to function, but unless social rules are given life by the moral sensibilities of individuals, they become ossified, and society degenerates into hypocrisy and ultimately corruption.

Jude the Obscure

Hardy's last novel is a grim and bitter attack on a society where rigid expectations of adherence to an externally imposed moral code repeatedly thwart and ultimately destroy both the central characters—Jude and the cousin he loves, Sue Bridehead. I introduce it into this discussion because the novel clearly distinguishes between an externally imposed morality about marriage and sexual relationships and the kind of moral sensibility that grows out of inner experience and conviction—that is, moral work.

Hardy shows both Jude and Sue struggling to find true expression for their own individual needs under the yoke of restrictive social beliefs about marriage. Initially, Jude takes social mores on trust, symbolized by the world of "Christ-minster" (Oxford), to which he longs to gain access but from which he is debarred by his low social position as a skilled artisan. Sue is far more rebellious: "The social moulds civiliza-tion fits us into", she says, "have no more relation to our actual shapes than the conventional shapes of the constellations have to the real star patterns" (p. 214). But, by the end of the novel, it is Sue who is swallowed up by a guilt-ridden adherence to convention, while Jude has seen through the charade.

The novel is, in a sense, the polar opposite of *Pride and Prejudice*. Where Austen, writing at the beginning of the nine-teenth century, envisages a harmony between individual and society, Hardy, writing at its end, portrays an almost irreconcil-able conflict between them. Despite this, Hardy's view of what really makes a successful marriage is surprisingly similar to Austen's. As in *Pride and Prejudice*, two other marriages are contrasted with the central relationship between Jude and Sue: one is a marriage based purely on "animal desire" (cf. Lydia and Wickham), the other is a marriage of empty convention (cf. Charlotte and Mr Collins). The difference is that both these other marriages also involve the central protagonists, and so attitudes towards divorce become one of the novel's main themes.

Jude, while still a callow and idealistic youth, is inveigled into a shotgun marriage with the sensual and worldly Arabella. The initial glow of sexual passion quickly fades, and he realises he is trapped in a loveless marriage to a woman who scorns his spiritual and intellectual aspirations. After a while the couple separate, and Arabella goes to Australia. Yet Jude's fervent belief in the sanctity of marriage convinces him that he must remain faithful to Arabella for ever. He moves to Christminster, where he meets and falls in love with Sue but feels unable to woo her because he is "licensed by the law of his country to love Arabella and none other unto his life's end" (p. 105). Sue's "uncarnate ideality" is in total contrast to Arabella's crude sensuality, and, throughout the novel, Jude struggles to find some reconciliation between the flesh and the spirit, both of which, by themselves, are shown to be inadequate and distorting to true human nature.

Social pressure, compounded by the revelation of Jude's previous marriage to Arabella, pushes Sue into marrying an older man, the teacher Philotson. Thus, Jude and Sue seem severed for ever. But the marriage is never consummated due to Sue's abhorrence of sex, and eventually she returns to Jude. But it is only with the re-appearance of Arabella that she is persuaded into a sexual relationship with Jude out of fear of losing him, and even when both of them have obtained a divorce, she still refuses to contract a legal marriage to him. She dreads:

> lest an iron contract should extinguish your tenderness for me and mine for you. I should be afraid of you, the moment you had contracted to cherish me under a Government stamp and I was licensed to be loved on the premises by you. [p. 267]

Yet by holding fast the freely chosen nature of their love for each other, Jude and Sue manage to create a happy-enough life together, despite the need to avoid the moralistic censure of those who disapprove of their chequered past and unmarried state. Their relationship is based on a love that, at its best, *unites* flesh and spirit, beautifying sex and corporealizing spirit. Unfortunately, Hardy's personal bitterness cannot allow the story to end there, and, inevitably, tragedy strikes with the murder of their own children by the mournful child of Jude's marriage to Arabella. Sue, riven by grief and guilt, conceives the idea that she has never really been divorced from her previous husband and, loveless or not, must return to him. She is now caught by the same "indissolublist" view of marriage from which Jude has painfully extricated himself.

Throughout the novel, Hardy is concerned with what constitutes a true marriage. There is a moment of supreme irony when Arabella returns from Australia and Jude, in despair about his relationship with Sue, ends up sleeping with her. Afterwards, he is filled with a sense of degradation. For although in the eyes of the law he is "licensed" to have a sexual relationship with Arabella and not with Sue, seen from the perspective of his own feelings in the matter the case is quite the reverse: he has, in effect, committed adultery with his legally married wife. Here, Hardy has deliberately set up a situation where a personal morality about fidelity is in direct opposition to social norms and expectations. Similarly, at the end of the novel, Jude pleads with Sue that their love for each other constitutes the true marriage, and the "social ritual" of her marriage to Philotson is an empty charade. Hardy thus repeatedly counterpoints a form of marriage (and fidelity) based on a real emotional bond (i.e. marriage-as-a-relationship) with one that is no more than a legalistic formality (marriage-as-an-institution).

While in Jane Austen's world individuals are able to fulfil their own needs within the framework of social expectation, in Hardy's world this is no longer possible. Social, moral, and religious expectations have become reified and divorced from the feeling life of personal need. This situation leads inexorably to tragedy and disaster. But Hardy's stout defence of the individual is very far from an argument that personal licence should replace Government licence. His critique only serves to underline the necessity of revitalizing the social with the care and compassion it currently lacks. With powerful irony, he portrays Jude's moral development in terms of a movement *away* from accepted mores, towards a morality hammered out on the anvil of his own personal suffering. Jude, the seeker after knowledge, discovers it is not to be found in the crumbling cloisters of Christminster but in contemplation of his own internal life. Hardy has a profound belief in the natural goodness of the human heart if it can be emancipated from the twin forces of animal nature and externally imposed morality. True morality must be in accord with personal feeling, but it is no less a morality for that. Indeed, it is more so.

Brief Encounter

Hardy's is a pessimistic vision in which ideals are shown to be merely illusory. Jane Austen, realist though she is, nevertheless maintains a strong commitment to the ideal world as the source by which the real world may be known and illuminated. She contrasts the world as it is with the world as we would like it to be. The central figures shine more brightly for being set off against others who are unable to achieve such perfection—in other words, others who are more like ourselves as we are. The same is true in a somewhat different way of *Brief Encounter*. The hero and heroine are ordinary people in an ordinary world but, like Elizabeth and Darcy, are also ideal types. Theirs is a truly romantic love story, and it is significant that it ends not in happy-ever-after fulfilment, but in a supreme act of renunciation by which they—and the audience—are transfigured, raised up towards an exquisite perfection from which all traces of the banal muddle, which normally intrudes into even our finest moments, have been expunged.

The trauma of moral conflict lies at the heart of the story, but, unlike Jane Austen, it is treated not as comedy but as tragedy. Moral work requires personal sacrifice and disillusionment but ultimately produces healing and renewal. Laura, the heroine (played by Celia Johnson) is a happily married woman. Her stereotypical middle-class marriage to Fred (who spends virtually the entire film doing the *Times* crossword) forms the backdrop for her unexpected love affair with Alec (played by Trevor Howard), a similarly happily married man. They meet by chance during Laura's weekly outings to the local town and fall violently in love, with a passion whose ardour is matched only by the anguish of their guilt.

All grand romantic passions contain this peculiar mixture of torment and joy. Popular notions of romantic love as happy-ever-after are, in fact, sentimentalized dilutions of the Romantic, which, by excluding the torment, deny the power of love and, in so doing, become escapist in a way that films like *Brief Encounter* are not. True, Laura's grand passion must have been the fantasy of many women in the dull suburban austerity of post-war Britain. These were the women whose daughters became feminists, fighting against the attitudes that kept women like Laura tied to the safe but limited world of home and children. But the film does not remain at the level of fantasy. Instead, reality and fantasy are continually contrasted against each other in the characteristic bittersweet style for which Noel Coward was famous.

After Laura and Alec have declared their love for each other, Laura is transported into a wild happiness. She travels home on the train imagining herself with Alec in a series of exciting—and glamorous—settings: in Paris at the opera, in Venice in a gondola, on a tropical beach at moonlight. Yet as she recalls this magical time, looking back from the end of the affair, her memory is shot through with compassionate irony: she thinks of herself as having been "like a romantic schoolgirl, like a romantic fool", fantasizing about being wooed and married to the ideal of her dreams. The scene counterpoints reality and fantasy throughout, most poignantly when the imagined palm trees of the tropical beach change into the pollarded willows by the canal and Laura gets off the train and walks home "quite soberly and without wings, without any wings at all". And, when she gets home, the journey that begun with such wild happiness ends with Laura deceiving her husand for the first time: "it started then—the shame of the whole thing, the guiltiness, the fear. . . ."

In this scene Laura realizes that the fantasies her love inspire can never be. This is the torment. Something at the heart of love, and not only adulterous love but any grand passion, runs counter to the possibility of its fulfilment. Reality is always an obstacle.

Throughout the film, the romantic excitement of the love affair is seen through the perspective of Laura's sadder but wiser reverie as she looks back from the disillusionment and pain of its ending. In turn, this reverie is set against the passionate yearning of Rachmaninov's second piano concerto on the one hand, and the prosaic world of husband and family on the other.

The declaration of love is one of the supreme moments in the conventions of romantic fiction, yet here it is interspersed with an interruption in Laura's reverie in which her husband, Fred, turns down the volume of the Rachmaninov on the gramophone. He tells her he will soon be finished with his crossword, and they can go to bed. Casually Laura replies, "Don't hurry, I'm perfectly happy" and then catches the significance of what she is saying. "If only it were true", she muses. "Not that anybody's ever perfectly happy really, but just to be ordinarily contented, to be at peace. . . ." Although she goes on to recall the time when she *was* happy, the audience already knows that this happiness is an illusion ("not that anybody's ever perfectly happy really"), which brings such pain as to make not perfect happiness but ordinary contentment the goal of her desire.

It is important that Laura is happily married. Even a happy marriage is no protection against the kind of love that Laura and Alec feel, because a happy marriage exists in reality. Fred is kind and understanding, but he is no romantic hero. Were Laura escaping from an unhappy marriage, the essential drama of her conflict would be weakened. What she is escaping from is that very sense of being "ordinarily contented" for which she now longs.

Laura and Alec are caught up in the longing for an ideal love. But the power of the film lies not in the lovers' fulfilment of the ideal but in their capacity to renounce it. Laura is tormented by moral considerations, some of which may sound quaint to many modern ears. When Alec says, "We know we really love each other, that's all that really matters", she replies, "It isn't all that really matters—other things matter—self-respect and decency. I can't go on any longer." But note that it is *self*-respect that Laura is concerned with. Although she lives in a social world in which infidelity is almost as deeply disapproved of as was Lydia's elopement in Jane Austen's day, it is not the respect of others that troubles her in the end but her own self-respect. She identifies with these social values because she identifies them with her concern for her husband and children. Ultimately she sacrifices love in the name of love, and, at the end of the film, this is gratefully acknowledged by her husband.

Fidelity to the ordinary is shown not to be dull and boring but noble and heroic. Responsibility to others, i.e. social needs, is shown to transfigure the lovers in a way that would not have been possible had they pursued their own personal needs regardless. Neither slavish acceptance of social expectations nor riding rough-shod over them can produce real personal development. What is required is a form of personal responsibility (that is, moral work) that acknowledges and respects both aspects. This is very similar to what Jung describes as individuation: "the aim of individuation", wrote Jung (1928, par. 269) "is nothing less than to divest the self of the false

wrappings of the persona on one hand [that is, social conform-
ity] and the suggestive power of primordial archetypal images
on the other"—in this case the archetypal longing for an ideal
love. This is why I earlier distinguished such longing from the
monogamous ideal. It is Laura and Fred who eventually achieve
the monogamous ideal through their acceptance that it is not—
and never can be—an ideal relationship.

Infidelity arises out of discontent. But the discontent can
often be due to inability to tolerate the state of "being ordinarily
contented". No matter how divine the discontent, it still involves the same deception and betrayal. As Laura says, "That's
what spoils everything". Yet her return to her marriage involves
equally painful disillusionment. She will never forget Alec and
will never be happy in quite the same way again.

Ironically, it is fidelity that provides the compensation for
this disillusionment. For the agreement to be mutually faithful
guarantees the specialness of the partner and of the relationship, and the need for this guarantee only makes sense in
terms of a recognition of their ordinariness. Descriptions of
marriage that gloss over its inevitable disillusionments therefore make infidelity *more* likely because they ignore what has to
be given up, which is, at bottom, the longing for divinity: that
is, divine omnipotence and perfection.

Madame Bovary

Madame Bovary tells the story of a woman who is unable to give
up this longing. Her insatiable craving for romance ends not in
renunciation but in her own destruction and, after her death,
the destruction of her husband and child. Here the real and the
ideal are contrasted in a quite different way. Madame Bovary
spends her entire life struggling against the dull reality of the
world as it is in favour of a world that can never be. She is never
able to accept the ideal world as an illusion whose purpose is to
enrich the real world, but seeks to do away with the real world
and put the ideal world in its place. There is no accommoda-
tion with the real world as there is in *Pride and Prejudice* and
Brief Encounter, but an implacable contempt for it as a mean-
spirited force that crushes everything noble and romantic.

Madame Bovary is not happily married. Her husband is a simple-minded petit bourgeois "whose conversation was as flat as a street pavement" (p. 54). As the daughter of a small-farmer, she had little choice in her partner but married the first man who took a shine to her.

> Before the wedding she had believed herself in love but not having obtained the happiness that should have resulted from that love she now fancied that she must have been mistaken. And Emma wondered exactly what was meant in life by the words "bliss", "passion", "ecstasy", which had looked so beautiful in books. [p. 47]

Flaubert himself is utterly contemptuous of the sort of gushing romantic novels his heroine was reared on, describing them as:

> this refuse of old lending libraries. They were all about love and lovers, damsels in distress swooning in lonely lodges, postillions slaughtered all along the road, horses ridden to death on every page, gloomy forests, troubles of the heart, vows, sobs, tears, kisses, rowing boats in the moonlight, nightingales in the grove, gentlemen brave as lions and gentle as lambs, too virtuous to be true, invariably well-dressed, and weeping like fountains. [p. 50]

Emma cannot reconcile herself to her dull provincial life and eventually finds a lover who seems to embody her romantic dreams. This man is in fact a cynical seducer, who deliberately plays the role of the romantic hero to suit his own ends. With savage irony, Flaubert chooses this character to express the romantic belief in the supremacy of the individual over the requirements of society:

> "Duty again!" said Rodolphe, "Always on about duty. I'm sick to death of the word. What a lot of flannel-waistcoated old fogeys they are, pious old women with beads and bedsocks, for ever twittering in our ears about "Duty, duty!" To feel nobly and to love what is beautiful—that's our duty. Not to accept all the conventions of society and the humiliations society imposes on us." [p. 157]

Emma is reluctant, but soon succumbs.

It is interesting to compare her immediate sensation with Laura's fantasy in *Brief Encounter*: for Emma there is no supervening moral consciousness to tell her she is being "a romantic fool".

> She was entering a marvellous world where all was passion, ecstasy, delirium. A misty-blue immensity lay about her, she saw the sparkling peaks of sentiment beneath her, and ordinary life was only a distant phenomenon down below in the shadowy places between those heights. [p. 175]

For Emma "was becoming a part of her own imaginings, finding the long dream of her youth come true". And this feeling also includes "gratified revenge" and "triumph" (p. 175). She seeks to obliterate the real world in a frenzy of hatred and frustration that gives her love a manic, desperate quality, driving her on to ever more extreme behaviour the more that reality threatens to invade. After a while her lover's true character begins to emerge:

> The grand passion into which she had plunged seemed to be dwindling around her like a river sinking into its bed; she saw the slime at the bottom. She refused to believe it. She redoubled her tenderness. [p. 183]

Eventually the love affair reaches its inevitable conclusion— her lover abandons her. Later she begins another affair, this time with a man apparently more "suitable"—so much so that he is presented as a man she might have happily married, had she had the opportunity. Yet this affair goes the same way as the last. Emma has become addicted to her romantic illusions and craves these beyond any actual relationship. Indeed, she uses them in order to maintain her denial of reality, running up huge debts, which are eventually called in. Unable to escape in any other way, she becomes frantic and swallows arsenic.

Flaubert detested the bourgeois world yet knew himself to be a part of it. "Madame Bovary, c'est moi", he said. Although it initially appears as if Emma is a victim of this unimaginative, small-minded, and socially restricted world that denies her the opportunity to express her obvious intellectual talents, it becomes increasingly clear that it is Emma who is destroying herself by her refusal to come to terms with its limitations. Her kind of happiness is an impossibility.

Conclusion

In the latter half of this chapter I have been suggesting that the continuing belief in fidelity is the expression of a moral social consciousness that recognizes the need to reconcile conflicting personal and social interests. But this reconciliation is itself an ideal state towards which individuals aspire. I have contrasted this moral ideal, expressed in *Pride and Prejudice* and painfully achieved in *Brief Encounter*, with the destructive disaster that accompanies the unchecked pursuit of romantic love in *Madame Bovary*.

I have also suggested that fidelity is not a given of relationships, nor can it be imposed by external demands for adherence to a strict moral code. *Jude the Obscure* shows the absurdities that result when legal institutional marriage is held in higher regard than the emotional bond that comprises it. Fidelity requires what I have called moral work, involving renunciation, sacrifice, and the toleration of disillusionment. As such, it becomes not merely a belief but an achievement. The difficulty of this achievement—for complex reasons with which I am daily concerned in my clinical work—seems to me the real reason why there is such a gap between belief and actuality.

Now the old outmoded certainties that Hardy fought against are being swept away, we need to be especially aware that all change brings both gains and losses. While individuals are free to pursue their own inclinations in the way that Hardy foresaw, it has also become difficult to find any moral bearings to guide behaviour. Rather than a procrustean moral code, we are in danger of having no moral code at all. It is no longer a question of needing to ensure that the personal informs the social, but one of remembering that the personal also needs to be informed *by* the social. The absence of social awareness constitutes the distinctive psychopathology of our time, namely narcissism, epitomized in the figure of Madame Bovary. Destructive attacks on social reality are no cure for destructive attacks on personal feeling.

A modern variant of such pathology is that typical film of the 1980s, *Fatal Attraction*. Neither the erring husband nor the one-night-stand lover is able to take responsibility for their actions, and the film descends into an orgy of gratuitous violence that offers no possible redemption. The all-American family is so threatened by its split-off impulses, projected into the lover who seeks revenge for the way she has been ditched, that its only recourse is to murder her before she murders them. There is no ennobling tragedy here, only a morally vacuous and mindless destructiveness.

It would therefore be a serious mistake to look at *Jude the Obscure* and think we know better now, let alone to imagine that the lovers in *Brief Encounter* would have been better off had they not renounced their affair. On the contrary, *Brief Encounter* illustrates how deeply personal acting in accord with social mores can truly be. We need to find a new way of addressing old certainties that have become discredited because of their oppressive aspect when divorced from personal feeling. The concept of moral work is an attempt to do this, linking post-psychoanalytic ideas of personal growth with an historical tradition of ethical concern. Jane Austen especially exemplifies the point that the progressive development of individual consciousness did not come into being with the creation of psychoanalysis, nor do I believe it will pass away if psychoanalysis is ever superseded.

On the other hand, even in Jane Austen's world it is only the exceptional individual who is fully capable of such development, recalling Jung's dictum that "Nature is aristocratic" and individuation is therefore not necessarily the path for all, far less a panacea (Jung, 1926). Laura's values of self-respect and decency also have their place here, as does the instinctive goodness of Jude.

The monogamous ideal is just that—an ideal. There is always a gap between ideals and the possibility of their realization in the world, but ideals are nevertheless necessary to give life meaning and value. They act as beacons pointing out the way, something to strive towards but never to reach. There is loss involved in recognizing this—indeed, it is the heart of tragedy—but it is far preferable to the futile and doomed attempt to deny the gap by omnipotent fantasy à la Madame Bovary.

Art and culture give expression to our ideal aspirations and are a crucial means by which moral values can be fostered and strengthened, not by didactic means, but by association with beauty and truth. Pluralistic values and life-styles greatly complicate this process, as does rapid social change. Yet despite all this it may still be possible to discern some common reference points, amongst a multiplicity of circumstances, of which fidelity may be one. In his poem entitled "Fidelity", D. H. Lawrence suggests that love can be compared to a flower that fades, while fidelity is like a gem that endures:

And man and woman are like the earth, that brings forth
    flowers
in summer and love, but underneath is rock.
Older than flowers, older than ferns, older than
    foraminiferae,
older than plasm altogether is the soul of a man under-
    neath.

And when, throughout all the wild orgasms of love
slowly a gem forms, in the ancient, once-more molten
    rocks
of the human hearts, two ancient rocks, a man's heart
    and a woman's,
that is the crystal of peace, the slow hard jewel of trust,
the sapphire of fidelity.
The gem of mutual peace emerging from the wild chaos of
    love.

CHAPTER SIX

Sexuality and the couple

Paul Brown

Uncovering sexuality

I t was on Monday mornings at 9 o'clock, nearly twenty-five years ago, that I ran my first clinic on the treatment of sexual difficulties. A car-worker from the then thriving industrial tracks of Coventry, having difficulties with his erectile capabilities, was the typical patient. His wife would probably be in a part-time job, also looking after three children, and he would be on a weekly shift pattern that every second week had him coming home after ten in the evening and every third week away all night. Treatment was often as much about re-ordering patterns of life and priorities as making diagnostic discoveries.

Nevertheless, it may be worth recalling, half an adult lifetime on, how revolutionary were the ideas and practices about the treatment of sexual difficulties that had just become available at that time. Masters and Johnson's work (1970) had just been published in the United Kingdom. For the first time in the history of clinical endeavour there was both a theoretical basis for the treatment of sexual disorders, firmly grounded in the observations of the psychophysiological laboratory, and a reasonably well described method of proceeding. No matter that there wasn't a terribly good match between some of the observations, some of the theory, and some of the treatment procedures that resulted. Until experience had been gained and some time had passed, it looked like a wonderfully integrated package. Coming as it did at the end of that extraordinary decade, the 1960s, clinicians had some of the power with which to approach and, indeed, radically affect for the better the sexual distress that many couples suffered.

Masters and Johnson made some startling observations, at least so far as clinicians were concerned. Perhaps the first was that sex tends to happen between two people! This followed through to the idea that a *couple* might be treated together, and by a couple; therapists were given permission to entertain the idea that a male and female clinician could join forces to explore sexual matters with a presenting partnership. That was an extraordinary idea.

The then Mrs Barbara Castle was indirectly responsible for the demonstration that having a male and a female therapist was perhaps more fun for the therapists than of long-term benefit to the patients. As Secretary of State for Health in the early 1970s, her Department was under pressure to provide free contraception. It went against her wishes, and a let-out was needed. It happened that Relate, then called the National Marriage Guidance Council, had just invited me to become Director of a project to see how the treatment of sexual difficulties within marriage could be integrated into the training of their marital counsellors. The research funding proposals for this project arrived in the Department at a time of political pressure for free contraception. As long as the researchers undertook not to use one-way screens, the Department of Health and Social Security said, the project would be funded. In announcing the funding, the Secretary of State was thereby in a position to make it clear that her Department was all in favour of sex within marriage, while neatly side-stepping the contraception issue. What that redoubtable lady would have done if she could have imagined that less than twenty years later Claire Rayner would be demonstrating the use of the contraceptive sheath, in glorious technicolour, on prime-time television, as part of the anti-AIDS campaign, I do not know. In due course Mrs Castle's successor, now Lord Ennals, announced the successful completion of the research pro-gramme (Hansard, 1977).

One of the outcomes of this three-year training and clinical study was not only that Relate was enabled to set up a nation-wide service for the treatment of sexual difficulties, but that we demonstrated that one therapist working alone could produce treatment outcomes that were just as good as those of two therapists working together—a finding that John Bancroft and his colleagues at Oxford also demonstrated at much the same time (Matthews et al., 1976). So Relate was fortunately spared the problems of having to find male and female therapists in order to staff the service that they had established.

Another startling observation that Masters and Johnson made was that the processes of human sexuality are normal. Sexual interest, arousal, and orgasm are the natural preroga-tive of the normal, intact adult human being. What we *do* with that capacity, and how we *use* it, and for what *purposes*, and in what circumstances, and how it might be regulated by law, is of course the subject of the human condition. But this observa-tion of Masters and Johnson should not be read amiss. When people presented with difficulties of sexual function, therapists discovered, after the first flush of enthusiasm for the new treatments, that the problem was not how to teach couples to function sexually. They possessed that capacity as of biological and maturational right, and as part of the divine complexity. The problem was how to help them stop stopping themselves.

The last startling observation that Masters and Johnson drew to our attention was the fact that the language in which we talk about sex is perhaps the greatest barrier of all to dealing with the subject. For most of us—and this includes clinicians—sexual experience is so private that even in our most intimate settings we may not have a language with which to convey our thoughts, wishes, or hopes. Indeed, we may not even *know* what it is we want to try to understand. The extraor-dinary ignorance that people have about their bodies continues to surprise. What is really happening to them in the exploration of their sexuality remains uncharted territory for many. "There be monsters here", the old maps used to say, as the unconscious still does for many.

Imagine being taught to drive in a darkened garage. You are not to be seen in public, lest you disgrace yourself. A board is put over the steering wheel, so that whatever knobs you touch and buttons you try to press is done by fumbling, not by sight. Let's imagine you have an instructor by your side, who assigns to the pedals some private names and lumps them in the general category of "those things down there". What goes on under the bonnet—the source of power—is not even mentioned, let alone how one might manage the energy that's there. And then let's imagine that you are let out on the road. We should see carnage all around us. Well—so we do in marriages where, for the most part, sexuality is supposed to be explored on the basis of the most profound misattributions.

In *Sex in Human Loving* (1973), Eric Berne set out to find a language in which to communicate matters sexual, and in doing so he described the essential dilemma for men and women in expressing their sexuality. This is what he says in describing the sexual organs.

> The sexual equipment of the male consists of two small crucibles, the testicles; each with its own still, the epididymis; and its own little [storage] tank, the seminal vesicle. These lead to a pump, the prostate, which delivers the product through a hydraulic ram, the penis. The female starts with the ovaries, which drop their ripened eggs like apples near the openings of the Fallopian tubes, whose gentle petals waft them down the tunnel towards the womb or uterus. The uterus is built to cradle the growing embryo and feed it into maturity. At the other end, the vagina is supplied with glands that lubricate to aid the brawny thrust of the penis as it slides down the ways ready to seed the new life with its seminal torpedoes. The vagina also has muscles that squeeze and pulsate and sweet-talk the semen towards its destination, the womb. Above [the entrance to the vagina] is the clitoris, an organ especially designed and supplied with nerves for exquisite titillation leading into ultimate ecstasy. In sum, then, the man has two exquisitely miniaturized cell factories and an aggres-

sive delivery system. The woman is well equipped to encourage and handle its deliveries, which she pillows in the most beautifully constructed incubator in the universe. She also has the equipment to nurse its grateful product.

But psychological complications arise because the man sticks out while the woman is tucked in, or, as someone said, the man has outdoor plumbing and the woman has indoor plumbing. Thus the man has built-in advertising which he can light up at night when occasion calls for it, while the woman can only do promotional work behind the scenes. It is something like the difference between a roadside hamburger stand with neon lights, and an elegant inn with the most discrete facade concealing its single downy chamber. [pp. 55–56] [—one to which the man forever tries to return and from which he is for ever excluded (P.B.)].

Here, in the last decade of the twentieth century, Masters and Johnson may be a starting point for modern thought, but perceptiveness about the human condition and its sexual frailty is not a modern prerogative. Montaigne, in his 1572 essay, *On the Power of the Imagination*, recounts the following:

I have personal knowledge of the case of a man who . . . had heard a comrade of his tell of an extraordinary loss of manhood that had fallen on him at a most inconvenient moment; and, when he himself was in a like situation, the full horror of this story had suddenly struck his imagination so vividly that he suffered a similar loss himself. Afterwards the wretched memory of his misadventure so devoured and tyrannized him that he became subject to relapses. He found some remedy for this mental trick in another trick; by himself confessing this weakness of his and declaring it in advance, he relieved the strain on his mind and, the mishap being expected, his responsibility for it diminished and weighed upon him less. When he had opportunity of his own choosing . . . he would have his virility tested, seized, and taken unawares, by previous arrangement with the other party. He was then completely and immediately cured of his infirmity. For once a man has been capable with a certain woman, he will never be incapable with her again unless out of real impotence. [Montaigne, 1572/73, p. 39]

As a description of anticipatory anxiety and its treatment, it is one that would grace the clinical literature. How fortunate the man was to having a willing partner.

Perhaps this is the central mystery of human sexuality—the willingness of one's partner. It not only encompasses the mysteries of the driven state that arises from human sexuality but also leads usefully into those areas of unwillingness and coercion that are at the heart of separation and divorce. Perhaps in legislation we could arrive at what is an essentially human— that is, psychological—view of the sexual process as expressed by the concept of sexuality and see how this might underpin changes in the present legal approach to these issues.

The mystery that is procreative in its intent, and which therefore carries the whole future of the human race, has been the subject of special interest by one means or another in every manifestation of human history. Christianity managed to associate guilt with the sexual act, and so with the idea of being a sexual person. Whether guilt is left as a concept or explored through the metaphors of psychoanalytic enquiry is perhaps not the essence of the matter. What is crucial is to try to come to decisions about what our sexuality is *for*. Then we might find some answers as to how its energies can be channelled.

Discovering difference

There is, of course, a central and irreducible paradox in considering human sexuality: the extraordinary *differences* between men and women. For the last thirty years or so it has not been fashionable to dwell upon these, as women throughout the Western world have provoked the process of what Teilhard de Chardin called "hominization"—their irrefutable claim to be persons of equal value to men in all aspects of existence, a claim that causes such anguish for some sections of the Anglican communion as the final barricades against the ordination of women are defended. But it is on the *differences* that there may be some value in dwelling. In the final analysis, sexuality is very much concerned with the interconnectedness of what goes on between the groins and between the ears relative to the procreation of the species. While since time immemorial it has been obvious that the groins are different, the evidence is accumulating rapidly that what goes on between the ears is remarkably different too.

It is an instructive exercise to try to imagine being a person of the opposite gender and looking out at the world through differently informed eyes. If you are female, try to imagine for a moment being male. Your fundamental task in the world—indeed, the only task that ensured you are here and that the species will continue to survive—is to penetrate the body of another person whom, by definition, you will never really know. If you are a man, imagine for a moment looking at the world through eyes that are conditioned by the act of welcome that is contained in the receiving of a lover. Forget for a moment whatever fears, doubts, anxieties, and social customs there may be; there is in the end no gainsaying the extraordinary differences that are contained in the complementary roles of the sexual act. Without both, neither would be complete. Yet with both, neither can be completely the other.

I was taught this in the space of a minute or two in some seminars on sexuality I was conducting for a Church group fifteen years ago. As part of one session I was listing the disorders of normal sexual function that occur, and assigning them to their categories—disorders of arousal, and so on. One category I referred to as disorders of penetration, and discussed within it the difficulties of the man who had a sudden loss of erection at the moment of insertion; and then began to talk about vaginismus—the term used to describe a spasm contraction of the muscles surrounding the vagina so that the entrance clamps up and insertion is impossible. It is a reflex to pressure upon the entrance as automatic as is the reflex blinking of an eye when a piece of grit hits its surface.

A lady broke the pattern of discourse. "I'm interested that you call vaginismus a disorder of insertion", she said. "From a woman's perspective, it feels like a difficulty of acceptance". Yet again one's entirely male perspective of the universe had led into fundamental error. And so it does, time and time again. The only way out that I know is to try to stay continuously open to the promptings of whatever is feminine within me, and learn from those I love what a language I hardly know would say.

The differences are not made any easier to comprehend when one considers that, as between male and female, the physiological processes of sexuality are essentially similar.

Cognitive processes influence the limbic system and other parts of the brain, providing the neurophysiological substrata of our sexuality. This system, in turn, influences the periphery via the spinal cord and reflex centres within it, which, via peripheral somatic and autonomic nerves, control genital responses as well as other peripheral manifestations of sexual excitement. Awareness of these responses completes the cycle (Bancroft, 1989, p. 13).

Masters and Johnson (1966) were among the first to demonstrate the essential similarity of the male and female system. In both men and women the early signs of sexual interest and arousal are an increase in blood flow. At a certain point in the male there are the beginnings of an erection. In the female there is the beginning of vaginal lubrication, which is the initial identical response in the woman to erection in the man. Not until Masters and Johnson had photographed the vagina under conditions of sexual arousal, now some thirty years ago, was this mechanism understood at all. It was thought until then that vaginal lubrication was either a drip from the cervix, or the product of two little glands, the glands of Bartholin, near the introitus of the vagina. Masters and Johnson observed the way that, as vaginal tissues became suffused with blood, there was an autonomic transudorific response across the vaginal membrane, creating the lubricating flow.

This led to immense changes in the treatment of sexual difficulties. Up until that time, many women experiencing difficulty with penetration had been encouraged simply to use some kind of cream to ease the act of penetration, which, of course, rested on the assumption that women did not really experience sexual arousal at all and were essentially involved in the sexual act for the man's convenience. But then we understood that to ask a woman to use cream to aid penetration when there was no excitement, and hence no lubrication, or none of the internal enlargement of the vagina that follows lubrication, was much the same as asking a man to tie a splint to his penis if there was no erection.

What differentiates men and women is the awareness of the experience. "Male and female created He them", says Genesis (1: 27). But as so often happens in crucial statements, the parentheses were left out. What happens in the brackets behind the statement? "That they might forever misunderstand each other"? However much flesh may be joined, there is a huge difference in the experience for one of depositing seed and for the other of the possibility of containing and nurturing new life.

Strictly speaking, the only natural uses for the sex organs are for making babies. Any other purposes are to some extent improper. Sex for pleasure, if contraception is used, is in some ways a biological betrayal. And yet these non-propagative uses of sex play a very important part for most people in everyday living.

We are the generation that has taken to itself the most extraordinary powers for separating the sexual and the procreative acts. Alex Comfort (1974a) observed some years ago that if one looks at the recorded history of Western civilization, there was, until the 1930s, no widespread questioning of the basic assumption that the sexual and procreative acts were fundamentally linked. He has called this the procreative view of sex.

Then, in the 1930s, stimulated to a large extent by Hollywood and the classic image of lovers going off into the sunset holding hands, together with the emerging sense of women demanding their own freedoms and rights within democratic systems, a view of sex began to appear that made it central to the quality of a relationship—what he called the relational view of sex. Perhaps the Abdication crisis and its causes also reinforced this view. It is around this time—the late 1930s—that we see the beginnings of the rise in divorce rates and the founding of the National Marriage Guidance Council, now Relate.

Then, with the advent of contraception in the early 1960s, comes a period in which sex is thought of primarily in terms of pleasure and fun—a recreational (re-creational) view of sex.

Medical technology has contributed hugely to this. From the capacity demonstrated from 1947 onwards to freeze and unfreeze sperm, the possibility of conception without a meeting of the human beings involved in any way at all (other than as re-constituted bodily fluids on a vitreous dish in a fertility laboratory) is now real. It is a long way from the days when the Royal College of Veterinary Sciences celebrated the Queen's Jubilee by unfreezing the sperm of a bull that had been stored in its cryogenic lockers in the year of her accession and impregnating a cow.

While science and technology march on, there are no essential advances of a similar kind in the basics of the human condition. Hatching, matching, and despatching are still the three main experiences of life. Not only have there been no essential advances, it is possible to assert without much fear of contradiction that there are unlikely to be any. There may be changes in form, but there will not be any in essential content. The need of human beings for each other will continue, whether that is expressed in the familiar institutions of marriage or in the less familiar yet rapidly rising Living Together Relationships that are already part of the American census record.

Towards a couples' charter

In spending time therapeutically in the struggles of other people's marriages, the question is frequently asked: "What *is* marriage, anyway?" If falling in love is what Freud described as a short-acting, spontaneously remitting psychosis, what are we left with when first passions have given way to the extraordinary task of sharing one's existence with another person, when lifetime commitments have accelerated in length beyond the wildest expectations of the prayer book, when selection is a very dicey business, and when divorce has taken the place of death as the means of creating all kinds of family disturbances—notwithstanding all the complications of choice rather than inevitability?

A couple recently asked me to commit to paper for them the assumptions I was using in working with them on *their* marriage. Rather than dodge the issue, I came up with the following:

- to make oneself available to the other person physically and emotionally, and thereby, through the reciprocity that that engenders, to discover to the best extent we can our own self, the mysteries of the unknown half of the world, and experience our own sexuality;

- to find ways of expressing ourselves through our children and set their boundaries whilst at the same time helping them find the ways in which they learn to express and become themselves and develop their own confidence in doing that.

What does it mean to "experience our own sexuality"?

I observed earlier that the central theme for the expression of sexuality within a lasting relationship is *willingness*—not only to experience oneself and make oneself available to a partner emotionally and physically, but also to explore the world through the other person's eyes and learn their language too. If, in the other management world that I inhabit professionally, the essential issues are to do with command, control, and co-operation, in marriage the issues are exactly the same but without a formal power structure. In consequence only co-operation really works, and that is the ultimate expression of willingness.

So, at its best, what happens to a person's sexuality in marriage? The answer is that it flowers. It is discovered, appreciated, enjoyed, shared, and explored through the richness of all five senses. At its best it is an aesthetic of sensibilities continuously refined.

That is all very well, you might say. "Nothing there that's going to rock the boat. Don't quite know what it actually *means*, but it's pretty strong on the feel-good factor."

Let me try, at least, to define some of the tasks.

In the first place, we need some much-improved cultural reference points. I should like to see someone do for sexuality what HRH The Prince of Wales has done for architecture—lift the subject to a level of interest and debate where standards can be explored. To my mind, the women's magazines have done a profoundly good job over the past twenty years of informing at least half the population about what is now known about sex. What I should now like to see is a debate that is not so much about the facts as the feelings of the process, and to see that increasingly enshrined in law. If one thinks what the Homosexual Law Reform Bill did in the late 1960s for one section of the population, I should like to see enshrined in statute some positive statements about the nature of human encounter, which might start:

• We hold it as self-evident that, through their differences, men and women create a unity and wholeness that is for the great benefit of themselves as individuals, the nation and the future of the human race. We therefore enshrine in this Declaration their interdependent equality as well as recognise their differences; and will strive in all our laws to ensure that these qualities are reflected as best we may.

In the second place, I should like the current campaigning, which stresses the dangers of sexual encounter, to be equally offset with public instruction about the benefits of good sex and sexuality well expressed. A major reason that the advertising campaigns on AIDS fail to hold the public mind or result in real changes in behaviour is that they take too little account of the common experience of sex, which, however fleetingly or unsatisfactorily, opens up the possibility of being whole. To try to convey simultaneously a message of the prospect of lingering death is to counter actual experience with too much distant catastrophe. In any event, campaigns that ask people not to do something, or in some ways reduce their pleasures, have an inevitable brake built into them. How much more productive might be a campaign that encourages the exploration of sexuality while setting it within a responsible framework. Jeffrey Weeks (1985) has observed that, so far as sex is concerned, in the natural tension between the rights of the individual and the interests of society, two models have alternated. One espouses repression, and the other liberty:

> If, as Krafft-Ebbing observed, "life is a never-ceasing duel between the animal instinct and morality", then an absolutist policy of sexual repression and control is seen as inevitable to guarantee civilisation. . . . If on the other hand sex is seen as a beneficient energy, distorted and perverted by the corruptive effects of a civilisation gone wrong . . .

then the possibility arises of a new freedom where men and
women walk in tune with their true natures. [p. 97]

Come back, Rousseau, all is forgiven! The difficulty arises in
deciding what is natural or unnatural, good or bad. Is sex
social in origin, or biological? If we reject one, are we forced to
accept the other? I doubt if either is itself sufficient to frame a
law. What the twentieth century has taught us above all else
about the human condition is the essential interdependence of
peoples. If this is true in a global framework, how much more
true is it in marriage—the setting that is the microcosm and
crucible of universal experience.

In the third place, and in part harking back to the first, I see
a need to try to find a new balance between the expression of
sexuality and personal statements of identity. If this part of our
century is about rejecting roles in favour of individualism, then
the search for individual identity through sexuality has to come
to terms with the corresponding *loss* of individual identity that
a marriage supposes in forming a joint identity. Willingness
comes back into play here, and the nature of partnerships.
Throughout our culture there is a huge amount of distress
occasioned by people—doctors, lawyers, and accountants especially—finding themselves in formal partnerships that are out
of joint with the times. Re-stating the nature of the contract
within commercial partnerships might have some very useful
spin-off for marriage—or, more interestingly, *vice versa*.

It has struck me recently, in struggling with the ending of
marriages, how little weight the law puts upon the original
commitment and how much it interferes at the points of breakdown. It is as if the implication were that people can be trusted
to enter into something but not trusted with its ending. Can
there be any other setting in modern society where people can
utter what appear to be binding statements and promises while
all the time there is a general expectation in the audience and
by the person administering either the sacrament or the public
duty of the marriage vows that there is hardly a fifty–fifty
chance of delivery?

The late Dr Mia Kellmer-Pringle of the National Bureau for
Co-operation in Child Care proposed that the law might take
account of two forms of marriage: one in which there are

children, and one in which there are none. In the latter, the parties should be as free to end their relationship as they were to enter it, so far as the law is concerned. It might require a solemn declaration of agreement to do so, and that would be that. Property issues apart, the State would have no interest other than its general concern for knowing what its citizens were up to.

When there are children, the response should be of a quite different kind. The birth of a child should contain within it the expectation that the parents had between them joint responsibilities that extended for at least a further 15 or 16 years; every aspect of the law should ensure that these are fulfilled. If divorce proved inevitable, for whatever reason—and it should be quite a difficult feat to accomplish—then by primary attachment of earnings, or whatever other device were appropriate, the continuing responsibility of the couple as parents would be made manifest. In such a way the law might move more towards the concept of responsibility than fault at the breakdown of a marriage that involves children. In England the Child Support Act of 1991 has at last enshrined a premise that there should be proper support for children following a divorce. Perhaps this might go some way towards avoiding the price of liberty for the grown-ups being the possibility of damage to the children.

A large number of marriages come to an end where one party is *unwilling*, as we know. From the Married Woman's Property Act of 1882 onwards, Parliament has nibbled at the dilemma as to how someone can be both an individual and a dependent. As a consequence of that Act, women have acquired the right to retain their assets and the right to receive support. What was of benefit to a privileged few created the case law for many. Equality at law became synonymous with sameness, not diversity. It is most people's observation that men and women are for all kinds of reasons *different*, but the law has tried to treat them as if they were the same. Perhaps it is time for the law to be framed within the concept of dissimilarities.

Where would that lead?

Perhaps one direction would be towards parallel law. The revision of employment law over the past 25 years has created a wide body of experience about how relationships can come to an end when one party is unwilling but where necessity, for whatever reason, dictates an ending. A manipulative ending of employment is enshrined within the concept of constructive dismissal. Both sides can be fairly clear in advance what the financial penalties attaching to that are likely to be, as is also the case with wrongful or unfair dismissal.

What would the outcome be if this type of law and experience were applied to the breakdown of marriage? Perhaps it would avoid the vast number of situations that try to pin fault and lay blame by recognizing that unfair things *do* happen, but that there are proper mechanisms for compensation. I am suspicious, as I suspect many lawyers are, of the many claims of unreasonable behaviour that appear as the basis for divorce. It is such a relative concept, and takes insufficient account of context. Marriage agreements should either be binding, solemn declarations, or they should include the option for an ending, with the financial and property consequences—as well as the consequences of having children—made thoroughly clear at the outset. Then we might move into an era in which the diversity of male and female is able to operate within an overall sense of security, to the great benefit of all.

CHAPTER SEVEN

Women, men, and intimacy

Susie Orbach

Gender relations in context

The last two decades have been such a tumultuous time for marriage and partnerships, particularly those between women and men, that it is now possible for an analysis of male–female relationships to be framed within the social sphere with reference to both the meaning of gender and the constraints imposed upon it.

With gender on the agenda, we, as people involved in intimate relationships, can now critique rather than reflexively act out sets of behaviours that coalesce around the category of gender. That is to say, we can assess the effect of sex-role stereotyping on our understanding of what it means to be a woman, of what it means to be a man, of what it means to raise children, and so on. It makes it possible for us to see with new eyes and speak with a different voice about the politics of intimacy.

The men and women who present themselves for couple therapy today and those who see them have been raised in similar and particular ways, with similar and particular sets of

111

expectations and similar and particular sets of desires from their partnerships. They/we have accumulated these ways of being through personal experiences within families of origin; through observations made about the partnerships of others—including the behaviours of men and women; through Hollywood; through Barbara Cartland, Norman Mailer, and their up- and down-market equivalents; and through the ideology of relationship that impregnates our cultural fabric.

The marriages or partnerships we are in, are wanting to be in, or are freeing ourselves from do reflect to a very great extent the values and images we have absorbed from those around us. That is not to say that we are all stamped out the same, or that we all want exactly the same thing in the same kind of ways, because manifestly we do not. It is to say, rather, that our desires, both conscious and unconscious, are structured in the context of what we deem to be possible.

The contract between men and women

What all of us grew up with—whether our own personal circumstances mirrored this model or not—and what we were taught to aspire to was a partnership in which the man would protect the woman, provide her with a home, provide her with whatever level of economic support he could (literally paying the bills or giving her housekeeping on a regular basis), and legitimate her sexuality through reproduction. The woman, in turn, would nurture, care for, and bring up the children and be responsible for the household labour and the domestic management of daily life.

Behind this essentially economic arrangement—an arrangement that was re-introduced in the aftermath of the rather different arrangements required by the Second World War—lay a complex set of emotional responsibilities that were as gender-based as the economic arrangements.

The emotional responsibilities ran thus: the woman was to do the emotional labour. She was to create the conditions under which a man's emotional life, often hidden from himself,

could be brought into their relationship. By keeping her anten-
nae highly tuned, she was to assess nuance so that she could
nurture him and provide the emotional refuelling that would
allow him to return to the workplace each day, confident in the
knowledge that his emotional worries were being sorted out
and that his children's problems, his children's needs, were
being catered for.

He knew that whatever challenges he faced at work, he
could expect his wife to back him up and to provide background help so that he could manage extra work, promotion,
moving around, or whatever. She, by furnishing these emotional services, would free him to fulfil an important aspect of
his masculinity—that is to say, his sense of independence, of
being a person with an agenda, with needs he could go after
and responsibilities he could meet. By a linguistic sleight of
hand that obscured the emotional work of his wife, he could
feel himself to be the one upon whom others depended
(Eichenbaum & Orbach, 1983).

His wife, on the other hand, could meet an important crite-
rion for the fulfilment of her femininity by being the giver
(Eichenbaum & Orbach, 1982). She was raised to provide these
emotional services—not, of course, that anyone ever put it so
crudely—without anticipating that there would be reciprocity.
Indeed, not only was it unlikely that this way of relating would
be reciprocated, it was likely that this part of her contribution
to the relationship would go unacknowledged and virtually
unseen. In other words, the woman's labour was often rendered
invisible, creating a situation from a woman's perspective that
describes and explains some of the difficulties that come up
between women and men, some of the deep misunderstand-
ings, the disappointments, and the unmet longings.

Many of us were raised in just such circumstances: the
woman doing the work of emotional relating, of connecting, of
keeping the affectional bonds; the man doing the work of providing economically and assuring himself of his independence.
He was needed because others needed him.

Nowadays we are all too aware of the kinds of problems that
arise when partnerships are constructed on this basis. And we
might think that today's partnerships are being forged on

rather different grounds. On enquiring about the love life of my 21-year-old niece, I received the response:

> "Oh, it is just so impossible these days. You don't know whether you are having a date or whether you are getting together for a business meeting. You don't know whether sex is on the agenda and how and who should make the first move. And if you are going to have a sexual relationship, then you have to worry about AIDS. You don't know whether you'll offend if you offer to pay, whether you'll offend if you don't. It was all so much easier in your day."

I empathized with her and chuckled to myself. I chuckled, not because of her predicament, which one could empathize with, but because of her notion—an entirely false one, I believe—that marriage and sexuality were stable categories until my generation came along and mucked it up for hers by divorces, women's liberation, contraception, and so on.

But I sighed, too, because what I had observed of younger partnerships, partnerships created in this apparently gender-conscious age, was that while much of the outside appearance had changed, while the women all had their own cheque books, credit cards, or child allowance, while their growing economic contribution to partnerships was being acknowledged, while who did the housework was a subject for negotiation rather than a foregone conclusion, while who initiated sex might vary, while who made decisions about where and how to live was discussed, reports from the emotional hinterland about the politics of intimacy seemed strangely stuck in the most appalling groove, wearing out the same record of the hidden dependency dynamic described above.

This is not to say, in any sense, that the social changes that have occurred are not important. They are. But they are not profound enough to create the kind of conditions in which partnerships between men and women will avoid the hurts, disappointments, and confusions that exist between them.

Is this an over-pessimistic reading of current trends in male–female relationships? On the one hand it is not, because the difficulties run deep. But on the other hand, if we can come to grips with this hidden emotional dependency dynamic, if we can take it out, interrogate it, look at it in ourselves, in our partnerships, in the partnerships of those we are working with, then the possibility is open to bridge the painful gulf that exists in so many couple relationships. We have a chance to connect, to create relationships that are vibrant, that include two emotionally aware people coming together.

So let us see if we can understand a bit more clearly these emotional dependency dynamics, and their interface with the problems that so often surround intimacy between women and men.

Dependency dynamics and their roots

Dependency dynamics are not simply learned as instructions, they are experienced early on in life. In the first relationship we all have (men and women), a relationship we could categorize as the very first love relationship, that between baby and mother (and I say "mother" as, for nearly all of us, that is how we were raised), the mother attempts to attend to the baby's physical and emotional needs so that the neonate can move from absolute dependence to becoming a person with felt agency through the process of separation–individuation.

Our first experiences of love and intimacy are ones in which we are the recipients of care—of, as Winnicott put it, "good-enough mothering". If we are lucky and all goes well, then we will grow up with a secure-enough sense of self, a sense of our own autonomy or subjectivity, and a sense of our connections—actual and potential—to the world around us. Intimacy will be an emotional situation we invite and savour.

But a mother's ability to respond to our needs depends upon many factors. It depends upon the level of economic support she has, the level of emotional support from husband or other family members, her own experience of being parented, and her belief system about how children should be raised and what it is that children need to know, experientially and actually, about intimacy.

If a mother is unable to *recognize* the needs of her child—*recognize* rather than *meet* those needs—two different kinds of things happen. On the one hand, the child, and later the adult, remains stuck in that very first attachment, still yearning for the kind of relating, the kind of contact that can give her or him sufficient emotional nourishment to grow into being autonomous. That person is then unable to move on to find recognition elsewhere and will instead seek it in relationships that contain, in nuance, aspects of that first most powerful relationship.

But, on the other hand, where needs have gone unrecognized, the developing psyche has to come to terms with this at some level. One of the ways this happens is that it takes into itself the idea that it is at fault, that its desires, its wants, its initiatives are somehow wrong. This feeling of wrongness, if acute (and I believe this applies to all of us along a continuum), creates a situation in which the developing person feels herself or himself to be unlovable, and to be insatiable. Such a person becomes afraid of his or her needs, which then become censored, split off (Fairbairn, 1952), or transmuted into a more manageable feeling, a feeling that renders the person less vulnerable, less at the mercy of the need, and apparently more in charge. But while the hurt is temporarily assuaged by removing agency or culpability from the object of desire by situating it within the self, this makes the person anticipate or approach relationships with a kind of hesitancy.

The first love relationship is the place where one learns most profoundly about relating, and insofar as that relationship is unsatisfactory, one compensates psychically by making up relationships in one's head, by having relationships with objects that are psychically and unconsciously manipulated—fantasy relationships, rather than actual relationships with others. One then both craves and fears relations of closeness with others. This helpless vulnerability scars a person's emotional memory, and yet he or she aches for a kind of merged closeness that can allow for truncated development processes to be released (Eichenbaum & Orbach, 1983).

One of the factors that is often overlooked in trying to understand psychological development is the impact of gender—the conscious and unconscious meanings of the mother's gender and the gender of the child she is raising—on adult male–female relationships.

Gender is a prism through which all of our lives are lived. It is ever-present and yet taken for granted. It affects the language we use (Tanner, 1991), the way we move, our conception of relationship (Chodorow, 1978, Gilligan, 1982; Miller, 1976), even the emotional states to which we have access.

In mothering a girl, a woman consciously and unconsciously guides her daughter towards taking responsibility for the care and nurture of others. She encourages her to be alert to the needs of others and to see a convergence between satisfying her own needs and meeting those of others. For many daughters this endeavour means that their own needs are converted or subsumed. Then her own unmet needs provide an emotional pool from which she can identify needs in others. Her femininity, her sense of self, is affirmed in a relational context in which she is giving (Eichenbaum & Orbach, 1982).

But her own needs for nurture can only be kept at bay in so far as she compulsively seeks narcissistic gratification in attempting to meet the needs of others. What she may be searching for is a relationship in which her needs are seen and met, in which her needs correspond exactly with the needs of the other, in which her self can merge with another and be cared for.

The picture is rather different for a boy. There is no imperative that he should give in this way, and there is no need for him to recognize that he is given to. Even if his needs are met as inconsistently as a girl's are (and I believe this to be the case), they are unlikely to be exploited in the service of caring for others. He is not required to learn this skill, because one day he will have a wife to turn to. The familial effort in his case is directed towards supporting his actions, his creations, to the mastery of activities rather than the making and preserving of affectional bonds.

Insofar as his needs go unmet or unrecognized, he may try to deal with his continuing desire for attachment not through the mechanism of closeness and merger, but through a denial of the need for closeness. In other words, he forges his masculine identity through the routes he has been given: through action, through the refusal to acknowledge affectional bonds, through a dis-identification with and differentiation from the feminine.

Father may be so frequently absent from the household because of his work commitments that he is unable to provide a positive model of identification in the young boy's struggle to differentiate from the mother. His physical and emotional relationship to the home is often distant, and insofar as the boy is able to use him as a source of identification, that identification may embody within it a distance from women, from mother, from the emotionally laden domestic sphere. For the daughter, meanwhile, father may be an exotic, feared, or loved figure (or, of course, all three). He is not only not like her, but she will not be like him. He then becomes a figure who is often too far removed for her to identify with when attempting a possible dis-identification from mother.

Dependency dynamics and intimacy in marriage

What does this mean when men and women attempt to achieve intimacy in adult heterosexual relationships?

Even if we are heterosexually orientated or directed, we hold inside ourselves the legacy of our first love relationship—a relationship with a woman. Insofar as this was a satisfactory experience, we have the possibility of achieving intimacy. Insofar as this caused difficulty, we are still—men and women both—searching for a more satisfactory relationship with a woman. Yet this relationship will be laden with the problematic emotional template of that first relationship.

If this analysis is accepted, we can go beyond the old paradigm that says girls marry their fathers and boys marry their mothers. We can see that, instead, to quite a large extent, everyone seeks to reproduce or repudiate their *first* relationship, and that intimacy for us all, closeness for us all, includes a re-encounter with the emotional tracings of early infancy and childhood (Clulow & Mattinson, 1989).

These emotional tracings include both the positive and the problematic aspects of that intimacy. For a man who had a difficult relationship with his mother, closeness with a woman may be threatening. He may seek to resolve this difficulty, as he did before, by bolstering his sense of difference, by creating distance, by retreating from a powerful maternal imago, which he now projects onto the woman he is at one and the same time attempting to be close to. He develops a stance of not needing, of requiring space and unlikeness.

The woman who has experienced a difficult relationship with her mother, on the other hand, may seek to solve the problems posed by this new possibility of intimacy by adhesion—by sticking herself to her partner, hoping that through intertwining their needs, her own needs will finally be met.

The man's attempt at distance and the woman's attempts at closeness thus clash, making the relationship, at worst, a battlefield. While she needs reassurance, he needs to deny his need of her. He needs her to express her neediness, and she needs him to negate his for her. This is such a common scenario that examples from my clinical practice and friendships abound. A clinical example demonstrates this dynamic clearly.

Mick, 58, is a loving man. He is very attracted to women who might be described as victims, to women who are apparently in great need. He flirts and attracts a good deal of female attention. But although he is quite secretive and demands his space and privacy, he is sexually faithful to his partner, Donna, and emotionally responsive to her. He says she is over-sensitive, that she sees what isn't there. Meanwhile he walks around feeling that he is secure in the relationship.

Donna, 52, grew up in the war and was extremely insecure. Over the years with Mick she has come to take in the love between them and feel strengthened in herself. For years their relationship was characterized by her fear that he would betray her, leave her, go off with another woman. She has mostly overcome this fear, but every once in a while it reappears with a vengeance. In the therapy, we have worked on her capacity not to see what is there, and to undo what is. She has come to a position where she feels relatively secure. She no longer worries that he is about to leave her, and she feels a kind of freedom to express autonomous, capable parts of herself that were previously hidden from both of them.

When these self-contained, autonomous aspects of self emerge for Donna, they are freeing and exciting, but they also produce a fear in her. She is taking a risk believing that she is loved, that all can be well in her relationship, that she doesn't have to fret and worry about it or squeeze the relationship this way or that in order to ensure its survival. In leaving "it" well alone, she has been able to enjoy the relationship and the security it gives her.

But what happens? After a few weeks of feeling like this, she takes a tumble. When we analyse what has occurred, we see that Mick has in some way provoked her or undermined her. Quite unwittingly, he is as scared of her display of autonomy as is she, and he finds ways to destabilize her, to stimulate her insecurity. He does this by being particularly secretive about his activities, by saying he must visit so and so because she is so lonely, by taking the 'phone in the other room when it rings, by leaving dangling between them a suspicion that there is someone else.

Mick is quite unaware of this behaviour on his part. But when we investigate it, we discover that without her articulation of her need he comes within a hair's breadth of feeling his own. This is a feeling that causes him such discomfort—as it resurrects his need for and dependency on a woman, a mother, the feminine—that he is compelled to shake it off, to pass the package of need back to his partner, to re-arouse her feelings of insecurity so that a status quo in which she is the designated needy one and he the need-free one is reinstated.

Their intimacy is then forged within a context in which there is a battle about who is to be the needy one and who the secure one, as though such emotional states could be parcelled up like possessions and tossed back and forth between them. The only possible resolution, beyond a continual reiteration of the cha-cha-cha, is for them to share the responsibility for the needs that exist between them, for both Mick and Donna to accept their individual insecurities, their needs for one another, their fears of intimacy, and to co-operate in not trying unconsciously to manipulate one another to do the emotional holding.

The situation is both similar and dissimilar in my work with lesbian couples. In woman-to-woman couples seeking therapy, I have noticed a familiar fear and contempt around the issue of emotional dependency and a kind of defensive positioning that seeks to outlaw this state as though it were dangerous. When the issue of who is holding the dependency and need in the relationship is raised, however, the shift to accepting that they might both be feeling needy is less resisted than it is in hetero-sexual couples. The main difference rests on the issue of merger. Both women feel drawn to adhere together, and the lack of gender difference often makes the creating of bounda-ries a difficult proposition. While the merger and love between the women may, in fact, heal some of the hurt and void each party has brought into the relationship, and so reverse some of the more painful legacies of the mother–daughter relationship, the issue of how to be attached and how to be autonomous can be a difficult one to negotiate without the boundary a gender difference so readily provides (Eichenbaum & Orbach, 1987).

In order for couples to confront the dynamic in which they either collude together to deny dependency or, in the case of many heterosexual relations, designate the woman to appear the needy one, individuals have to confront the fear and con-tempt they hold towards the notion of dependence. They need to struggle through to recognizing that, far from being a human failing, dependency is part of the definition of what makes us human. To be human means to be connected to others, to rely on them, to communicate with them, to share with them, to create together. In this we are unlike other species, for our mutual creations and our interdependence mean that we do more than reproduce what is—we don't make the same nest again and again—we create the conditions under which it is possible for us to change, to make anew the conditions under which we live.

But as long as we remain unaware of the processes that keep us from being intimate, as long as we conspire together to treat need and dependency with contempt, we are condemned in our marriages and partnerships to repeat the gulf between men and women as members of a sex, and men and women as individuals.

If we can dare to put the issue of dependency on the agenda, if as practitioners and partners we can scrutinize our own feelings about it, our own prejudices, and our own fears, if we can see that insatiability is a defence against the exposure of need and that distance is likewise, then perhaps we can risk peeking in and seeing what is so awful about need, about dependency. We may find, as many couples in therapy have been able to, that we then secure what we require. Exposing dependency needs may make it possible for them to be recognized and met rather than squashed by denial or displays of insatiability.

CHAPTER EIGHT

"Good-enough" marriage

Christopher Clulow

The chapters in this book have highlighted the multi-dimensional nature of marriage, mapping out terrains of personal and social histories in an attempt to take stock of this institution-cum-relationship. The ground has by no means been fully covered. Other chapters might have attended to marriage as a legal contract, an economic unit, or an anthropological phenomenon. Perhaps it is significant that the common thread running through this book is the concept of marriage as a personal relationship. There are problems with this emphasis, especially when the personal is disconnected from its social context, but there are also opportunities stemming from it.

Eileen Bertin indicated the scope for personal and social learning that marriage affords in the Prologue, an aspect to which I referred in chapter one when reviewing what functions marriage might have in contemporary society. Martin Richards and Penny Mansfield highlighted opportunities for reconstructing marriage, personally and socially, in the struggle to reconcile belief systems and experience. Michael Sadgrove referred to the redemptive possibilities in marriage, by which he meant not a passive surrender to something greater than oneself but active engagement in a task resembling that described by Warren Colman, writing from a psychological perspective, as "moral work". Paul Brown called for a positive affirmation of sexuality in its fullest sense, a statement of intent that might be enshrined in public declaration or statute. Susie Orbach addressed the developmental implications of men and women achieving what she has described as "emotional literacy" in their relationships. These are just some of the ways in which the work of marriage has been thought about in this book. But the question remains, why is *marriage* necessary?

It is precisely because private arrangements have social implications (especially when there are children) and because social systems have implications for the arrangement of private life that marriage would have to be invented if it did not already exist. That does not necessarily mean it would be invented in its present form; but it is to acknowledge the gate-keeping function of marriage between the worlds of personal and social meaning that, together, regulate relationships between men and women. What we are witnessing is the endeavour to re-think marriage in ways that resolve some of the contradictions and problems highlighted by present conditions. In that sense we are engaged in a collective process that is not so very different from that which challenges couples in the course of their own marriages. Conflicting views are only to be expected insofar as the process, like marriage, is concerned with balancing the pull of conservation with the push of change.

A central "condition" of present-day marriage is the expectation of companionship. As a concluding thought, I want to ask what factors have a bearing on the quality of relationship in marriage when an important part of its purpose is to provide mutual help and comfort, to be the primary source of emotional support for partners and a means of discovering and affirming personal identity—"person making", as the process was referred to by Michael Sadgrove, and something that is quite distinct from conferring identity by the status passage of a wedding ceremony. With a view of marriage as both social environment and expression of identity for partners, I want to ask what yardsticks we have for assessing the state of a relationship, and to do this with reference to what is known about healthy functioning in family relationships rather than by drawing inferences from relationships that have run into difficulties.

Health in relationships

Donald Winnicott, a child psychiatrist and psychoanalyst, coined the adjective "good enough" to describe the qualities of parenting that facilitated the healthy development of children (Winnicott, 1971). It is a template that can usefully be transferred to marriage. What is a "good-enough" marriage?

Health, in Winnicott's terms, is both a relative and a relational concept. It cannot be assessed in isolation from the context in which a person lives, yet it hinges on the kind of relationships people have with themselves as well as with others. The mother/infant relationship provides the object of much of Winnicott's thinking and the context within which key maturational processes occur. The foundations for ontological security are laid down in that relationship as the infant experiences, tests out, and revises his sense of the distinctions and connections between "me" and "not me", what lies within and what lies without, the world of meaning and the world of experience. These processes can only occur if the environment, provided first by the mother and later by others, is "good enough". This implies, initially, a high degree of identification by the mother with the infant (what Winnicott describes as "primary maternal preoccupation"), which allows her to know about and be responsive to his wishes, but also provides him with an experience of otherness so that he comes to believe in and relate to an external reality that transcends his omnipotent fantasies.

The notion of there being inner and outer worlds with different realities is not confined to psychoanalysis. The dramatic arts at one end of the spectrum and nuclear physics at the other share a respect for subjective realities and relativity, as well as a healthy regard for the so-called "real world". In the object relations tradition of psychoanalytic thought, John Bowlby spent most of his working life researching the processes by which individuals acquire their inner world models, fuelled by the powerful drive to form and sustain attachments to specific and significant others. An interesting illustration of these processes is contained in Bowlby's biography (1990) of the naturalist Charles Darwin. In this he provides graphic examples of the influence of transference, that temporally unbounded relationship, on adult relationships at home and at work, underscoring the influence childhood experience can have on a person's physical and emotional well-being throughout life.

The degree of congruence between inner models and outer realities, which determines their reliability as guides for predicting and responding to the behaviour of others, can be taken as one yardstick for measuring health. High degrees of congruence endow people with a positive sense of self-worth and with a capacity to trust others and to make predictions that turn out to be well-founded. These provide the foundations that enable individuals to venture out with confidence on all kinds of enterprises, unimpeded by feelings of anxiety, suspicion, or fear that have no basis in reality. Low degrees of congruence, on the other hand, can severely restrict the capacity for social involvement and result in mental and physical ill-health.

Winnicott (1971) was quick to point out that his concept of health is not the same as happiness:

> The life of a healthy individual is characterized by fears, conflicting feelings, doubts, frustrations, as much as by positive features. The main thing is that the man or woman feels he or she is living his or her own life, taking responsibility for action or inaction, and able to take credit for success and blame for failure. [p. 6]

Health is intimately connected with feeling alive:

> Health . . . includes the idea of tingling life and the magic of intimacy. All these things go together and add up to a sense of feeling real and of being, and the experiences of feeding back into the personal psychic reality, enriching it, and giving it shape. The consequence is that the healthy person's inner world is related to the outer or actual world and yet is personal and capable of an aliveness of its own. [p. 9]

He goes on to list the capacity of the healthy person to be alone (by which he meant the ability to be alone in the presence of another; he was not referring to solitude), a capacity for concern (which he linked with a sense of guilt and the wish to make reparation), and a tolerance of health towards ill-health, which comes from an integrated personality.

In his summit values Winnicott describes attributes that closely resemble Maslow's (1970) "self-actualizing" people. Maslow depicts individuals as having an hierarchy of needs, starting with basic physiological needs (food, sleep, sex), moving on to safety needs (protection, security, predictability), the need to belong and to be loved (affectionate relationships), esteem needs (involving self-respect as well as status in the eyes of others), and, finally, the need for self-actualization. Although his basic thesis sees people satisfying lower-level needs before moving on to those of higher levels, he does envisage interchangeability between the different levels (for example, one level serving as a channel for gratifying other higher or lower levels of need).

For our purposes, his theory is less interesting than the characteristics he ascribes to self-actualizing people, who are, by his standards, the healthiest of individuals. He describes these people as being motivated by "being values" (Maslow, 1971). They are integrated (there is no splitting between sexual and affectionate relationships, no work/joy dichotomy), they have a sense of living firmly inside their own skins but are also involved in causes outside themselves, they are open and can abandon themselves to experience but will not be swamped by group pressure, they can listen to themselves as well as to other people, they recognize the choices open to them and accept responsibility for the course they take, and so on.

One of the problems of assessing mental health in individuals is that the descriptions often come without reference to what they have to do. However much we might agree with Maslow's descriptions, they do lack a context, other than a normative view of the meaning of life. They can imply a static notion of health, one that is regarded as the outcome of a linear process of development. The differential impact of life events, and the almost infinite variety of meaning that can result from the personal interpretation of social, material, physical, spiritual, and environmental experience is played down. In short, emphasis is placed on an ultimate goal of human development rather than upon process, on the destination rather than on how the journey is managed—a journey in which there is much to-ing and fro-ing between different positions of health and ill-health, maturity and immaturity, integration and fragmentation.

Although individuals can be said to have inner relational systems, the task of assessing health in individuals and their relationships becomes a little easier when outer relational systems are taken into account. It is then possible to ask for what purpose two or three people are gathering together, and to assess the quality of their relationships in connection with carrying out that purpose. For example, one indicator of emotional health for couples is the degree of success they have in bringing up children.

In the 1970s, some research was conducted in the United States into what constituted "healthy" families (Lewis et al., 1976). A family systems perspective was used in the research, and the endeavour was to identify the characteristics of family systems that produced healthy children.

In assessing the families in their sample, the researchers looked at five variables that governed interactions between the members. First was the power structure. In their white, middle-class, North American sample of the late 1960s, they deemed healthy families to be those that had a clear hierarchy, where the parents had a viable coalition, the leadership usually resting with the father (although this was not always so, and in many cases leadership would move between the parents according to what had to be done). Family members related in an affiliative way. This last was the most striking of the characteristics linked with healthy power structures and family relationships generally. A confident expectation that others would be responsive encouraged involvement, openness, and an outgoing manner in relationships.

A second yardstick was the degree to which families encouraged the process of individuation. The ability of family members to express themselves as feeling, acting, valuable, separate individuals, their capacity to respect the unique experiences of others and to manage a permeability in their relationships that enabled them to hear and respond as well as to speak and assert, were all marks of health. Members did not speak for each other, there was a minimum of absolute beliefs, and patterns of dominance and submission were not brought into play to resolve disagreements and disputes.

A third measure was the capacity of families to accept separation and loss. This factor was critically related to the flexibility of the family system, influencing how well it could adapt and change over time to take account of the different developmental needs of members and the demands and challenges of the world outside. Flexibility was connected not only with success in coping with past losses, but also with the links that members had with others outside the family circle. Those who had an identity that reached beyond the intimacy of family life were less dependent upon a confined group of people for meaning in their lives.

A fourth indicator concerned perceptions of reality. This links with the earlier discussion about degrees of congruence between inner and outer worlds. Healthy families were apt to see themselves as others saw them. Their "mythologies" were congruent with each other and functional in their dealings with the outside world (which did not necessarily mean that family members shared the same stories). These families were not locked into a particular phase or episode of their history; they accepted the passage of time, and they behaved appropriately within the context of their cultural system.

The final variable concerned affect—the ways family members expressed and handled feelings, and the emotional atmosphere within the group. It will come as no surprise to learn that healthy families had a well-developed capacity for empathy and sustained a prevailing mood of warmth and mutual concern. This minimized the amount and intensity of conflict.

As the title of their book suggests, the Timberlawn researchers saw no single thread leading to health in family relationships. Instead, they identified some of the interconnecting variables that came together within the contexts of history, culture, and social class to be represented as healthy. But their identification of affiliative attitudes—respect for their own subjective experiences and those of others, permeable interpersonal boundaries, flexibility, high levels of personal initiative, and tolerance towards the autonomy of others—resonates with what one might expect to find in good partnerships. Moreover, the study drew attention to the qualities of marriage best suited to the healthy development of children—a good "fit" between the different skills of parents, pride in each others' capabilities, no strong competitive pressures, sufficient affection for there to be no need for emotionally charged alliances with members of the opposite sex either outside the family or with one of the children, and so on.

How do these reports from the worlds of psychoanalysis, humanistic psychology, and systems theory link up with the concept of "good-enough" marriage?

Maslow postulated that human behaviour was motivated by an hierarchy of needs, ranging from the most basic—for physical survival—to the quest for transcendent meaning in life. Those most at risk were those whose basic needs were not being met, a view supported by statistical evidence that marital instability is associated with social and economic deprivation. Psychoanalysts of the object relations school place emphasis on relational rather than material factors in defining the nature of human need and the building blocks for healthy development. They argue that the most fundamental human drive is to form and sustain attachments with others. Winnicott took the mother–baby relationship as the central paradigm for the facilitating environment in which this drive finds expression and in which the infant's need is recognized, if not satisfied. In his view these were preconditions for social and emotional development. He left the door open, however, for other partnerships to continue the process. The Timberlawn researchers provide evidence of the marital partnership acting in this capacity and signify the critical part played by the parental couple in promoting the healthy development of all family members, most notably the children; healthy marriages were those where parents felt their emotional needs were sufficiently well met not to have to become inappropriately involved with their children.

From this perspective it is possible to conceive of marriage as having two key psychological functions, which, in turn, create yardsticks by which the health of a relationship can be measured. In the first place, marriage exists to provide an environment in which the social and emotional development of individuals can continue in adult life. Secondly, it is there to supplement the resources of individuals and free them to participate in the wider arena of community life. The two functions are intimately connected. It is difficult, if not impossible, for people to give to others what they have not received themselves; conversely, stability and continuity in partnerships provide the springboard for wider enterprises.

Marriage, when working well, can provide partners with support, companionship, stimulation, and challenge. It can also help them be, in Winnicott's terms, "good-enough mothers" to each other. This "mothering" process takes place at conscious and unconscious levels and is not what common parlance might assume it to be. Some further explanation is required.

Marriage as a facilitating environment

From the outset, psychoanalytic insights into marriage have paid particular attention to the unconscious contracts that operate between partners, contracts designed to manage shared anxieties (Bannister & Pincus, 1965; Dicks, 1967). The prospect of intimacy constitutes a universal anxiety. Because it is both feared and craved for (there is a fundamental ambivalence that attaches to involvement with others because of the threat to the sense of self), couples work out defensive arrangements to manage conflicts that are principally concerned with the need to be attached, the need to be separate, the fear of loss or rejection, and the powerful feelings that surround the ontological agenda. This can result in different kinds of marital dance—the stylized tango, the entangled waltz, the detached jive, the narcissistic pirouette, the shadowing cha-cha-cha—each designed to find a comfortable balance between distance and proximity.

Mattinson and Sinclair (1979) describe three patterns of defensive interaction that regulate the marital "dance": "Cat-and-dog" partnerships enact an oppositional stance designed to preserve distance in a rigid and uncompromising way; this, while frustrating the wish to be close, provides some protection from anxieties associated with intimacy. "Babes-in-the-wood" partnerships depict another kind of inflexible arrangement, one designed to play down or avoid difference and separateness except in relation to those outside the dyad. "Net-and-sword" partnerships depict polarized, but potentially complementary positions, reminiscent of the psychologist Jung's (1926) container–contained pattern of interaction.

Different couples feel comfortable with different degrees of distance at different stages of their relationship. The task of establishing a partnership often requires a closeness and exclusiveness that would be unsupportable later on, when the partners have children or other responsibilities. Some flexibility and capacity for change is required, which involves being able to live with the feelings and anxiety engendered by relocating oneself in relation to others. Healthy characteristics that permit such movement have been described by Ruszczynski (1992) in relation to couples seeking help as:

> a capacity for healthy ambivalence which would allow them each to acknowledge their part in the marital problem; a reasonable capacity to deal with anxieties; a capacity for concern for the other; a capacity to take back projections fairly easily; and a sense of psychological separateness as well as a commitment to the relationship. . . . Further, such couples would have some capacity for containment as individuals as well as having successfully created a containing marital relationship. Such couples could be said to be interacting within a constellation of defences and object relations of the depressive position and be deemed to be psychologically reasonably healthy. [p. 41]

While all marriages are defensive, in the sense that they preserve and need to preserve difference in order to make relationships viable, they also provide opportunities for contact between partners and with the self in the partner. It is when defences and personal boundaries are so rigid as to make individuals impermeable to themselves and others, or when they are organized so as to make them overpermeable, that problems arise.

It is important to add that interpersonal boundaries are violated in good marriages; indeed, there can be no development without the positive outcome of processes of projective identification. Here is a crucial link between Winnicott's "handling", "holding", and "object-introducing" function of the "good-enough mother" and Bion's concept of containment (see Brooks, 1991, and Colman, 1993, for a comparison). Bion extends Winnicott's "holding" function by focusing on the unconscious transactions between mother and baby, with the mother being open to the experience of her child, receiving and containing projections, and offering back an experience that diminishes the infant's anxiety, thereby increasing his or her capacity to be alone within a relationship.

What happens between parent and child can also occur between partners. Marriage has been described as the "direct heir of childhood relations" (Thompson, 1960) because of a central truth: within every adult remains a child who is searching for expression. The opportunities for physical and emotional intimacy within marriage can excite that child into life, bringing unmet needs, unresolved conflicts, and unfinished business from past families into present-day partnerships. At an unconscious level, partners may communicate with each other about these matters in the primitive, preverbal way that an infant does with a receptive mother: he or she is made to *experience* what the other is feeling yet cannot form into a thought or put into words. If this experience can be received and contained by the partner, made safe enough to be brought into awareness and handed back, so to speak, less emotionally charged, there is huge potential for modifying inner representations of the world to come into line with current realities; in other words, there is great scope for personal and social learning to take place. Projective systems, as well as being self-protective, then function as a means of communicating about and managing fundamental areas of anxiety.

With this model, the measure of a "good-enough" marriage is not necessarily the way that partners treat each other as recorded by the outside observer (who may only be witness to the end product of a good marriage, to the process of working one out, or to an image the couple wishes to convey about themselves), but the capacity of the relationship to contain the different and complex layers of communication and interaction that take place between them.

The success of individual partnerships depends, in turn, upon how facilitating the environment is for marriage to operate in a "good-enough" way. Here, the wheel turns full circle and encompasses issues raised in the preceding chapters.

A common thread running through all the contributions in this book, and one that is perhaps surprising given their emphasis on relational matters, is the recognition given to environmental factors for the success or otherwise of the private venture of marriage. Attaching significance to the environment of marriage is a far cry from the call that is sometimes heard for a return to Victorian family values. The image of that period as a golden age of the family is as remote from reality as the rose-tinted images held by some of those who long for marriage but have yet to experience it. However, there are indications that the pendulum regulating the balance between private and public aspects of marriage may have completed an arc and be on the turn. This is not to predict the greater regulation of marriage by State or Church, but simply to recognize that marriage is an open system. As such, it can hold up a mirror to what is happening in the relationships between men and women in other sectors of society. Given this reality, rethinking marriage is an enterprise that extends well beyond the confines of the private world of the couple.

REFERENCES

Archbishop's Commission (1971). *Marriage, Divorce and the Church.* London: SPCK.

Askham, J. (1984). *Identity and Stability in Marriage.* Cambridge: Cambridge University Press.

Austen, J. (1813). *Pride and Prejudice.* Harmondsworth: Penguin Classics, 1985.

Bancroft, J. (1989). *Human Sexuality and Its Problems* (Second Edition). London: Churchill Livingstone.

Bannister, K., & Pincus, L. (1965). *Shared Phantasy in Marital Problems.* London: Institute of Marital Studies.

Berne, E. (1973). *Sex in Human Loving.* Harmondsworth: Penguin.

Berger, P., & Kellner, H. (1964). Marriage and the Construction of Reality. *Diogenes:* 1–23.

Billig, M. (1992). *Talking of the Royal Family.* London: Routledge.

Blumstein, P., & Schwartz, P. (1983). *American Couples.* New York: McGraw Hill.

Bowlby, J. (1990). *Charles Darwin: A New Biography.* London: Hutchinson.

Britten, V. (1929). *Halcyon or the Future of Monogamy.* London: Kegan Paul.

Brooks, S. (1991). Bion's Concept of Containment in Marital Work. *Journal of Social Work Practice*, 5 (2): 133–141.

Brown, P. (1988). *The Body & Society*. New York: Columbia University Press. London: Faber, 1989.

Buber, M. (1959). *I and Thou* (trans. Gregor Smith). Edinburgh: T. & T. Clark, 1970.

Burgess, E., & Locke, H. (1945). *The Family: From Institution to Companionship*. New York: American Book Company.

Byng-Hall, J. (1986). Resolving Distance Conflicts. In: A. Gurman (Ed.), *Casebook of Marital Therapy*. New York: Guilford.

Carr, W. (1985). *Brief Encounters*. London: SPCK.

Chodorow, N. (1978). *The Reproduction of Mothering: Psychoanalysis and the Sociology of Gender*. Berkeley, CA: University of California Press.

Churton Braby, M. (c1909). *Modern Marriage and How to Bear It*. London: Werner Laurie.

Clulow, C. (1984). Sexual Dysfunction and Interpersonal Stress: The Significance of the Presenting Complaint in Seeking and Engaging Help. *British Journal of Medical Psychology*, 57: 371–380.

Clulow, C., & Mattinson, J. (1989). *Marriage Inside Out: Understanding Problems of Intimacy*. Harmondsworth: Penguin.

Collard, J., & Mansfield, P. (1991). The Couple: A Sociological Perspective. In: D. Hooper & W. Dryden, *Couple Therapy*. Milton Keynes: Open University Press.

Colman, W. (1993). Marriage as a Psychological Container. In: S. Ruszczynski (Ed.), *Psychotherapy with Couples*. London: Karnac.

Comfort, A. (1974a). Sexuality in a Zero Growth Society. In: R. Francoeur & A. Francoeur (Eds.), *The Future of Sexual Relations*. New York: Prentice Hall.

Comfort, A. (1974b). *The Joy of Sex*. London: Quartet Books.

Corbin, M. (Ed.) (1978). *The Couple*. Harmondsworth: Penguin.

Countryman, L. (1989). *Dirt, Greed and Sex*. London: SCM Press.

Crowlesmith, J. (1951). Spiritual Values in Marriage Guidance. *Marriage Guidance*, June.

Davis, G., & Murch, M. (1988). *Grounds for Divorce*. Oxford: Clarendon Press.

Dicks, H. (1967). *Marital Tensions*. London: Routledge and Kegan Paul. [Reprinted London: Karnac Books, 1993.]

Dominian, J. (1967). *Christian Marriage*. London: Darton, Longman and Todd.

Dominian, J. (1968). *Marital Breakdown*. Harmondsworth: Penguin.

Dominian, J. (1981). *Marriage, Faith and Love*. London: Darton, Longman and Todd.

Dumon, W. (1991). *Families and Policies: Evolutions and Trends 1989–1990*. European Observatory on National Family Policies. Brussels: Commission of the European Communities.

Eichenbaum, L., & Orbach, S. (1982). *Understanding Women: A Feminist Psychoanalytic Approach*. Harmondsworth: Penguin.

Eichenbaum, L., & Orbach, S. (1983). *What Do Women Want? Exploring the Myth of Dependency*. London: Michael Joseph.

Eichenbaum, L., & Orbach, S. (1987). *Bittersweet: Love, Envy and Competition in Women's Friendships*. London: Century.

Elliott, B. (1991). Demographic Trends in Domestic Life, 1945–1987. In: D. Clark (Ed.), *Marriage, Domestic Life and Social Change: Writings for Jacqueline Burgoyne*. London: Routledge.

Fairbairn, R. (1952). *Psychoanalytic Studies of the Personality*. London: Tavistock Publications.

Flaubert, G. (1857). *Madame Bovary* (trans. A. Russell). Harmondsworth: Penguin, 1950.

Furlong, M. (Ed.) (1984). *Feminine in the Church*. London: SPCK.

General Synod (1978). *Marriage and the Church's Task*. London: CIO Publishing.

Gibran, K. (1926). *The Prophet*. London: Heinemann.

Giddens, A. (1981). In: K. Knorr-Certina & A. Cicourel (Eds.), *Advances in Social Theory and Methodology*. London: Routledge and Kegan Paul.

Giddens, A. (1991). *Modernity and Self Identity*. Oxford: Polity Press.

Gilligan, C. (1982). *In a Different Voice*. Cambridge, MA: Harvard University Press.

Gottman, J. (1991). Predicting the Longitudinal Course of Marriages. *Journal of Marital and Family Therapy, 17* (1): 3–7.

Green, M. (1984). *Marriage*. London: Fontana.

Haldane, D. (1991). Holding Hope in Trust. *Journal of Social Work Practice, 5* (2): 199–204.

Hampson, D. (1990). *Theology and Feminism*. Oxford: Blackwell.

Handy, C. (1990). *The Age of Unreason*. London: Arrow.

Hansard (1977). *Parliamentary Debates*, 23 March (p. 578). London: HMSO.

Hardy, T. (1895). *Jude the Obscure*. London: Macmillan, 1968.

Hayter, M. (1987). *The New Eve in Christ*. London: SPCK.

Holloway, R. (Ed.) (1991). *Who Needs Feminism?* London: SPCK.

Housden, R., & Goodchild, C. (1992). *We Two*. London: The Aquarian Press.

Jung, C. (1926). Marriage as a Psychological Relationship. In: *The Development of the Personality. Collected Works, Vol. 17*. London: Routledge.

Jung, C. (1928). The Relations between the Ego and the Unconscious. In: *Two Essays on Analytical Psychology. Collected Works, Vol. 7*. London: Routledge.

Kiely, G. (1984). Social Change and Marital Problems: Implications for Marital Counselling. *British Journal of Guidance and Counselling, 12* (1): 92–100.

Lawrence, D. H. (1929). Fidelity. In: J. Fuller (Ed.), *The Chatto Book of Love Poetry*. London: Chatto and Windus, 1990.

Lawson, A. (1988). *Adultery: An Analysis of Love and Betrayal*. Oxford: Blackwell.

Lewis, C. (1960). *The Four Loves*. London: Geoffrey Bles.

Lewis, J., Beavers, W., Gossett, J., & Phillips, V. (1976). *No Single Thread. Psychological Health in Family Systems*. New York: Brunner/Mazel.

Malan, D. (1979). *Individual Psychotherapy and the Science of Psychodynamics*. London: Butterworth.

Mansfield, P., & Collard, J. (1988). *The Beginning of the Rest of Your Life?* London: Macmillan.

Marris, P. (1992). The Social Management of Uncertainty. In: C. Parkes, J. Stevenson-Hinde, & P. Marris, *Attachment Across the Life Cycle*. London: Routledge.

Maslow, A. (1970). *Motivation and Personality*. London/New York: Harper & Row.

Maslow, A. (1971). *The Farther Reaches of Human Behaviour*. Harmondsworth: Penguin.

Masters, W., & Johnson, V. (1966). *Human Sexual Response*. London: Churchill Livingstone.

Masters, W., & Johnson, V. (1970). *Human Sexual Inadequacy*. London: Churchill Livingstone.

Matthews, A., Bancroft, J., Whitehead, A., Hackman, A., Julier, D., Gath, D., & Shaw, P. (1976). The Behavioural Treatment of Sexual Inadequacy. *Behavioural Research and Therapy*, *14*: 427–436.

Mattinson, J., & Sinclair, I. (1979). *Mate and Stalemate: Working with Marital Problems in a Social Services Department*. Oxford: Blackwell.

Medoff, M. (1982). *Children of a Lesser God*. London: Amber Lane Press.

Miller, J. (1976). *Towards a New Psychology of Women*. Boston: Beacon Press.

Montaigne, M. de (1572/73). *On the Power of the Imagination* (trans. J. Cohen). Harmondsworth: Penguin Classics, 1958.

Morgan, D. (1992). Marriage and Society: Understanding an Era of Change. In: J. Lewis, D. Clark, & D. Morgan, *Whom God Hath Joined Together: The Work of Marriage Guidance*. London: Routledge.

Nyrgen, A. (1932). *Agape and Eros* (trans. A. Hebert). London: SPCK.

Phillips, R. (1988). *Putting Asunder: A History of Divorce in Western Society*. Cambridge: Cambridge University Press.

Pincus, L. (Ed.) (1960). *Marriage: Studies in Emotional Conflict and Growth*. London: Institute of Marital Studies.

Powell, A. (1971). *Books Do Furnish a Room*. London: Heinemann.

Raschke, H. (1987). Divorce. In: M. Sussman & S. Steinmetz (Eds.), *Handbook of Marriage and the Family*. New York: Plenum Press.

Reibstein, J., & Richards, M. (1992). *Sexual Arrangements: Marriage and Affairs*. London: Heinemann.

Richards, M., & Elliott, B. (1991). Sex and Marriage in the 1960s and 1970s. In D. Clark (Ed.), *Marriage, Domestic Life and Social Change: Writings for Jacqueline Burgoyne*. London: Routledge.

Russell, W. (1988). *Shirley Valentine*. London: Methuen.

Ruszczynski, S. (1992). Notes Towards a Psychoanalytic Understanding of the Couple Relationship. *Psychoanalytic Psychotherapy*, *6* (1): 33–48.

Scarf, M. (1987). *Intimate Partners: Patterns in Love and Marriage*. London: Century.

Scruton, R. (1986). *Sexual Desire: A Moral Philosophy of the Erotic.* New York: Free Press.

Shils, E. (1981). *Tradition.* London: Faber.

Stein, M., & Moore, R. (1987). *Jung's Challenge to Contemporary Religion.* Wilmette, IL: Chiron Publications.

Stevenson, K. (1982). *Nuptial Blessing.* London: Alcuin/SPCK.

Stone, L. (1992). *Road to Divorce; England 1539–1987.* Oxford/New York: Oxford University Press.

Tanner, D. (1991). *You Just Don't Understand: Women and Men in Conversation.* London: Virago Press.

Tanner, T. (1972). Introduction to: *Pride and Prejudice.* Harmondsworth: Penguin Classics, 1985.

Thomas, D. (1954). *Under Milk Wood.* London: J.M. Dent & Sons.

Thompson, G. (1960). Introduction to: L. Pincus (Ed.), *Marriage: Studies in Emotional Conflict and Growth.* London: Institute of Marital Studies.

Van der Post, L. (1976). *Jung and the Story of Our Time.* Harmondsworth: Penguin.

Van de Valde, T. H. (1928). *Ideal Marriage: Its Physiology and Techniques.* London, Heinemann Medical Books.

Van Gennep, A. (1960). *The Rites of Passage.* London: Routledge and Kegan Paul.

Wallerstein, J., & Blakeslee, S. (1989). *Second Chances. Men, Women and Children a Decade after Divorce.* London/New York: Bantam.

Weeks, J. (1985). *Sexuality and its Discontents.* London: Routledge and Kegan Paul.

White, K. (1992). "The Social Significance of Marriage." Paper given at St George's House, Windsor Castle, 8 February. [Unpublished.]

Winnicott, D. (1971). The Concept of a Healthy Individual. In: J. Sutherland, *Towards Community Mental Health.* London: Tavistock.

INDEX